THE INDIAN WORLD

DIMITRI D. LAZO

THE INDIAN WORLD

David Kopf
C. James Bishop

FORUM PRESS

THE WORLD OF ASIA SERIES

WILLIAM J. MILLER, Consulting Editor
St. Louis University

THE SOUTHEAST ASIAN WORLD

JOHN F. CADY
Ohio University

THE JAPANESE WORLD

WILLIAM J. MILLER
St. Louis University

THE INDIAN WORLD

C. JAMES BISHOP
Manchester College

DAVID KOPF
University of Minnesota

Published simultaneously in Canada.

Printed in the United States of America.

Library of Congress Catalog Card Number: 77-81185

ISBN: 0-88273-503-9

Cover Design by Mike Whitney and Barb Hueting

Contents

Preface

THE INDIAN WORLD is a brief survey textbook designed primarily for use in Asian and world civilization courses. The text has been written to give the student with little experience in Indian history a broad image of the cultural, social, political, and geographical forces which have shaped contemporary India.

THE INDIAN WORLD analyzes the making of modern India primarily within a political framework. The volume focuses on the political processes as it evolved in India over the past three centuries. The history proceeding the arrival of large numbers of European peoples in the Indian Ocean area has been surveyed cursorily with major attention reserved for an explanation of South Asian development under the impact of European expansion. Space limitations have necessitated a brief discussion of the development of the British Empire. Of primary concern is the explanation of how the British affected the traditional values, institutions, hopes and aspirations of various social and political groupings in South Asia. Particular attention has been concentrated on the national drive for independence.

The authors feel that this text would be of value to study groups which might wish to know more about one of the areas of the world that has been a major center of civilization for 4000 years and more.

The authors acknowledge their indebtedness to a number of people who helped this project to completion. Many thanks are due Pamela Claeys, Patricia Nightingale, Rhonda Pilcher, and Kay Sprugeon for typing the manuscript. Thanks are due Irene and William J. Miller for their aid in compiling the index. In addition, Professor Miller gave unstintingly of his time in order to bring to fruition a volume and project whose basic plan was initially his, and his devotion has measurably improved the finished project. Professor John F. Cady also helped considerably in shortening the text without sacrificing clarity and content. Grateful appreciation must be extended to Dorothy L. Ilgen of Forum Press, for she provided the editing talent which the authors feel made the narrative more lively and succinct.

In addition, Professor Bishop expresses his deep appreciation to his wife and mother, two devoted people whose encouragement, support, and love helped turn his interest in the East into a profession rather than an avocation.

C. James Bishop

David Kopf

Introduction

LIKE EUROPE, INDIA is more than a nation; India is a subcontinent, rich in tradition and diversity. Few, if any, modern states contain within their borders the cultural and linguistic pluralism that to India has been a way of life for thousands of years. The slogan adopted by the Republic of India, "Unity in Diversity," is a living testament to the richness of this phenomenon. But diversity to the contemporary Indian has been both a blessing and a curse. It has encouraged tolerance but made planning difficult; it has deepened the religious experience but frustrated education; and it has enriched the cultural legacy while retarding technology. Many observers, especially those from the West, have attempted to develop an appreciation for and an understanding of this diversity by comparing it to a yet unborn United States of Europe. They argue that within the proposed states, united under one hegemony from Dublin to Vienna and Oslo to Rome, there might be found (within one political framework) an equivalent of the cultural pluralism and ethnic diversity that seems to have long existed within the confines of traditional India. While the Europe-India comparison could probably be duplicated by artificially creating states in other global areas, the fact remains that more than a little historical understanding can be gained through thinking of India as a geographical or cultural entity rather than as a nation per se.

India, like Europe or the Middle East, is a region through which many different peoples have passed and left behind a legacy that survives in the present. It is a land where people speak at least fourteen major languages and more than one hundred major dialects. The *Census of India* enumerates well over 1,000 mother tongues present in the republic today. This type of pluralism staggers the minds of inhabitants from states whose nationalism is based, at least in part, on linguistic homogeneity; and it is not uncommon for people to question whether a system composed of what appears to be an endless variety of parts can in fact endure. Some, particularly Westerners, have written volumes arguing it cannot. But time has proved the prognosis wrong. India can survive as a free and independent state. Why? How? The answers are to be found in her history.

1

The Making
of Traditional India

AS CAN BE SEEN FROM the map on page 33, India is a subcontinent of Asia. The Indian Ocean, which borders nearly half of India, has provided effective insularity from people living to the south of the subcontinent. Although Romans and Arabs interacted with Indians by sea, migrations, military excursions, and even cultural influences did not generally come to India via waterways. The only exception to this general rule occurred after the arrival of the Europeans in India. The Europeans destroyed the relative maritime isolation by converting the Arabian Sea and the Bay of Bengal into vehicles of change in both a military and a cultural sense. However, this development came long after the arrival of the Portuguese, the Europeans who arrived first in 1498. Generally speaking, the water which surrounds much of India has served as a protective shield rather than an avenue of entrance. Likewise the mighty Himalaya Mountains on the northeast border of India have served as a nearly impregnable barrier, as have the jungle lands on the Burmese side, though the jungle appears to have been far less formidable a shield than the mountains.

• Geographic Factors

Peoples, ideas, religions, and other significant influences have come to India by one main route: over the northwest passes of the Hindu-Kush Mountains. These and other lesser mountain ranges, which today comprise the Afghan-Pakistani border, extend along the northwest rim of the subcontinent on approximately a forty-five-degree angle; they run from the Arabian Sea to Kashmir, where they join with the Himalayas. Though the ranges of the northwest form a clearly discernible border, they are unlike the impregnable Himalayas, which average well over 20,000 feet in height. The mountains of the northwest are fairly easily scaled in some places, for they contain three or four major passes through which migratory peoples, including conquerors, have passed since the beginnings of recorded history. The most famous of these passes, the Khyber, has facilitated the passage of large numbers of nomadic tribes, mostly from Central Asia, who have come, settled, and been rapidly assimilated into the social structure on the Indian plains below. A case in point would be the Rajputs, a group of tribes who are believed to have migrated from Central Asia to the area north of Bombay over 1200 years ago. Once in India these migrants were assimilated rapidly, and they have been considered the cream of Hindu militancy and afforded high rank for a millenium or more.

Seldom have incursions through the passes caused cataclysmic confrontations or destruction. Usually assimilation has been rapid, perhaps because the newcomers always constituted a minority and the indigenous majority simply made adjustments which incorporated emigrants into the general milieu. But occasionally conquerors with superior organization and weaponry have poured down through the mountain passes leaving death, destruction, and change in their wake. In the last 4,000 years this has happened at least twice: once around 1500 B.C. when an Indo-European nomadic and pastoral people known as the "Aryans" imposed their sway (and their civilization) and again around 1200 A.D. when Turkish-speaking armies professing the Muslim faith established an Islamic state in north India. But these invaders, both of whom appear to have originated beyond the Hindu-Kush Mountains, never obliterated the existing civilization, no matter how they tried. The conquerors simply added another level of diversity or enrichment to that which already existed. Thus waves of intruders found their place in Hindustan (place of the Hindu) much as waves of conquerors found their places and identities in Europe after centuries of acculturation and adjustment. India and Europe share a common history of migration, conquest, and assimilation, though India probably never experienced conquest as destructive as that of Eastern and Central Europe in the thirteenth century when hordes of Mongols swept across half of Europe.

The sea and the great mountain ranges of the north are not the only topographical features that have helped shape contemporary India. Equally important are the two great rivers of the subcontinent, the Indus and the Ganges, for it is on the plains through which these rivers flow that most of India's history has been written. It would be difficult to overestimate the importance, particularly to the Aryan north, of these two river systems. Their water and silt have played a major role in the agriculture, transportation, and industry of the region. On their plains have flourished all of India's major empires, and the bulk of the socio-religious patterns have been clearly tied to these rivers and their tributaries. The River Ganges, which flows parallel to the Himalayas, is the most sacred as well as the most productive of India's rivers. Varanasi (Banaras), the Jerusalem of India, is located on its banks; and the adjacent plains can be compared to those of the Egyptian Nile in terms of fertility and productivity. Also the long stretches of monotonously flat plains through which the Ganges and the Indus flow have encouraged unity in the north, while the short rivers of South India, which flow through rocky terrain, have encouraged the opposite. All the great dynasties of India, especially those capable of unifying, were North Indian in origin, and their expansion always followed the paths carved by these two river systems.

No discussion of the historical importance of topographical formations would be complete without reference to the Deccan Plateau. The Deccan exists in the form of a triangular table, bounded on the north by the Vindhya Mountains and on the southeast and southwest by the Eastern and Western Ghats, ranges small in height but large in importance. Between the Ghats and the sea are narrow stretches of land, nearly 500 miles in length, that have harbored self-contained city-states whose identities developed quite apart from one another, as well as apart from India as a whole. And finally, between the lower end of the Deccan Plateau and the southern tip of the subcontinent lies a large, beautiful, and productive area known as Tamilnad. Here in the land of the Tamil many a civilization has flourished, and it may well be that the pre-civilized culture of the inhabitants predates that of the north. Certainly the languages of the south, called Dravidian, are different from those of the Aryan north. The Dravidian languages are not derived from Sanskrit as are north Indian languages. The Deccan itself has played a significant role historically. This large plateau, which rises 3,000 to 5,000 feet above the plains below, has most often resisted invasion, be it from the north or south, Christian or Muslim, foreign or indigenous. The Deccan separates the Aryan north from the Dravidian south, and because of its rough terrain it has a life style that, while very Hindu, is different from that which thrives at the lower levels.

• Regionalism as a Factor in Polity

Historically the Indian subcontinent has been united administratively but not culturally. India's first universal state dates back to the third century B.C. with the rise of the Maurya dynasty. India, like Europe, has seldom known true cultural unity. The imperium of a Charlemagne or a Napoleon has appeared as seldom in Europe as it has in India. The great difference is that most of India is today one political entity, whose leaders are attempting to rule and coordinate all regions within one centralized framework, while Europe has remained a patchwork of relatively small states. The problem of unity is often geographical, not cultural. As C. Collin Davies has argued, "One of the most important lessons of Indian history is that a united India was impossible until the development of communication after 1857 facilitated centralization." Before the development of railroads and the telegraph, it was impossible to join together the lands north and south of the Vindhya Mountains. A few rulers like Muhammad bin Tughluq, Asoka, and Aurangzeb did conquer the Deccan and add it to their Gangetic-based empires, but their rules represented little more than temporary military decisions. Distance and terrain made conquest difficult and consolidation impossible. Armies from the north could penetrate the Deccan, but the logistics of communication taxed the northern empires beyond their abilities. Thus the Vindhya range, which virtually cuts India into two parts, traditionally served as a dividing line — politically, culturally, and linguistically. Technology before the British era was not sufficient to hold together an area as large as India. But while the 2,000 miles that India extends north to south has been difficult to unite because of distance and the Deccan terrain, the 1,500 mile east-west direction has offered far less resistance.

India north of the Vindhya is popularly termed Aryan India, while the area south of the range is known as Dravidian India. This classification is not entirely accurate, but it is useful as a guideline. Regionally speaking, there has existed in the subcontinent for 3,000 years a northern region, the culture and language of which are closely tied to Sanskrit, the tongue spoken by the Aryans who conquered India in the second millenium B.C., while in the south there has existed for at least that long a civilization or culture known as Dravidian. Thus the Aryan north and the Dravidian south for thousands of years have existed as great cultural and linguistic blocs, separated by the mountainous, impoverished, and under-developed Deccan hinterland.

India is, however, not divided simply into the threefold division of Aryan, Deccan, and Dravidian so often described in older textbooks. Within the three divisions are to be found strong regional identities that may have greater call on the allegiance of inhabitants than do the larger divisions. None of the three classic divisions has ever really enjoyed unity, except perhaps the northern one. Northern India has known political unity more often than the other two, but none has experienced unity often or for long durations. Political unity has been the exception more than the rule. What unity has existed is more a product of language and culture than of political structures. Also most of the regional identifications of South Asia developed in a pre-technical age when even small political aggregates were difficult to sustain. Thus most regionalism in South Asia is tied to language and ethnic groups, and understandably so.

If one keeps in mind that most of what is described as "nationalism" in the West is built around ethnic or linguistic groups, then regionalism in India becomes more easily understood. What is called regionalism in South Asia is termed nationalism in Europe. If Europe (or at least most of it) were united under one or two governments, what is now termed German nationalism would become German regionalism. If India were to break up into fifteen or twenty sovereign states, what is today termed regionalism would tomorrow have to be called nationalism. This is because the borders of most of the twenty states which today comprise the Republic of India coincide with the linguistic realities. Regionalism in India appears to be clearly tied to language patterns, for much of the political energy of India over the past two or three decades has been directed at nothing more than making state boundaries coincide with linguistic ones. And though the Centre (meaning national) government has opposed movements designed to bring the two in line, it has time and again acquiesced rather than risk the threat of civil strife and dismemberment.

• The Culture of the Gupta Period (320-ca. 500)

After the Mauryan Empire, the second great era of political unification occurred under the dynasty of the Gupta (320-*ca.* 500), the classical age of Hindu India, although waning Buddhism and Jainism also made their contributions. At a time of unmatched cultural splendor as well as imperial grandeur, the heart of the new empire lay in northern India around the Ganges Valley. The zenith of its glory was attained in the reign of Chandragupta II (375-415). The Guptas gave India a magnificant period of civilization, comparable to the Periclean Age in Greek history, but largely confined to the privileged classes.

The Gupta patronized the flowering of literature in what became the golden age of Sanskrit, the sacred language of the Brahmins. For instance, the epic poem, the *Mahabharata*, was recast and put into its present form. The court encouraged gifted writers, who developed a significant secular literature — undoubtedly the eminent poet and playwright, Kalidasa, best personified this era. His poetry portrayed love, nature, and legends of the gods and their consorts, while ignoring the dreary side of life, since poets were forbidden to mingle with those of lower caste. Usually recited at court, Indian poetry of this period emphasized beauty of language rather than intellectual content. Cultural historians have long regarded Kalidasa also as the Shakespeare of Sanskrit drama. The aristocratic classes enjoyed these plays (or *nataka*) performed at court, local temples, or for private groups, which were often presented in conjunction with religious functions, like the miracle plays of medieval Europe. Stages utilized little scenery or few props, but dance themes and hand gestures (*mudras*) were important. Stories concerned love affairs, humorous romantic mixups, and improbable social blunders, with happy endings to conclude the frolics. *Sakuntala*, Kalidasa's most popular play, has been long admired in the West. A veritable storehouse of children's tales — fairy stories and animal fables (especially the *Panchatantra*) — flourished and then made their way to the Mideast and Europe.

Art reached its classical period inspired by religious themes, both Buddhist and Hindu. The Buddha images found at Sarnath, near Banaras, constitute some of the finest sculpture still found in India. Buddhist sculpture sought somewhat to dehumanize the Buddha and strip away individuality in line with his teachings. This trend stressed a rigid mask-like face with chiseled eyes, mouth, and eyelids. Artists consider the most famous Gupta paintings to be the frescoes adorning the walls and ceilings of the Ajanta caves (about 200 miles northeast of Bombay), representing Indian court life and episodes in the life of the Buddha. Many scholars regard these works to be the climax of the achievement of Indian art. Shortly after the Guptan age, another pinnacle in cave temple artistry was attained at Ellora with the magnificant Kailasanatha, carved out of the side of a mountain. As for Gupta architecture, there remains nothing comparable to the foregoing, although a few rock-cut Hindu temples have survived the ravages of later Muslim and Hun invaders. Artists and craftsmen, however, proved their skill in metallurgy. The pillar at Delhi, made of wrought iron, is a marvel of artistic achievement in this field. Casting copper figures of the Buddha climaxed with one statue eighty feet in height created at Nalanda.

Classical Hindu music and dance, currently of great interest in the West, flourished under Guptan patronage. The mastery of King Samudragupta (*ca.* 330 — *ca.* 375) in music and song was commemorated by the coins and medals of the period, which depict him seated on a couch playing the Indian lute or *vina*. Again religion (Buddhist and Hindu) helped to spur artistic genius. The traditional Indian musical scale was heptatonic (seven-toned), and the improvisational character of Indian classical music, following a complicated set of formulas called *ragas*, is surprisingly modern by Western standards. Musicians could, by improvisation, set the emotional mood and philosophic interpretation of the performances. Dance forms appeared in a new Sanskrit text book, explaining the significant hand gestures and movements of the classical school of Hindu dance, each with its particular message and symbolic meaning.

Science and technology developed medicine, mathematics, chemistry, and astronomy, influenced to some degree by Greek elements. The outstanding university at Nalanda (with its eight colleges and three libraries) attracted students from all over Asia. Indian physicians understood the structure and function of the spinal cord and the complexities of the nervous system, combining this knowledge with consummate skill in bone-setting, plastic surgery, caesarian delivery, and other medical techniques. Objection to dissection, however, prevented further advances. Mathematicians introduced so-called "Arabic numerals," the zero, and the decimal system, later adopted by the Islamic world and transmitted to Europe. The techniques for using square and cube roots as well as the formulation of the relation of the diameter to the circumference of a circle (pi=3.1416) were marvelous products of Indian knowledge. Chemistry and metallurgy advanced the tempering of steel and iron and the processing of dyes for exotic fabrics. Arabs and Europeans eventually perfected both techniques. The Arabs named one Indian fabric *quittan*, hence the word cotton. *Calico* comes from Calicut, the Indian city, while the terms *chintz, cashmere, madras,* and *bandanna* are also Indian. Astronomy copied the Greeks, but its advances were not especially noteworthy.

The wealth of the Gupta attracted many traders and visitors from abroad. Especially attractive to them were the silk textile industries of Bengal and Banaras and the cotton cloth of Mathuria. Contacts with the West and East increased rapidly. Land routes through Persia carried goods to the West. Roman gold paid for Indian pepper, indigo, jewels, and spices to such an extent that the successors of Emperor Nero, fearing the drain on precious metal, took measures to restrict the trade.

The intensity of overseas exchange made the city of Ujjain a bustling commercial center, situated as it was at the convergence of many arteries. Seeking further commercial advantage, numerous Indian colonists sailed eastward to Burma, Malaya, Borneo, Java, Indochina, and Ceylon to establish settlements. Kambuja (Cambodia) represented one of the most significant areas of colonization, where there were several successive Hindu

Gometeshwara, Sravanabelgola. Government of India Tourist Office, Chicago.

dynasties. Among these were the Khmer kings, who around the year 1100 erected the magnificent temple of Angkor Wat. Built to honor the Hindu goddess, Shiva, its galleries are adorned with scenes from Hindu epics — certainly one of the most resplendent religious monuments ever created by man and a tribute to Gupta traditions.

Even China and India maintained close relations during the Guptan period for one of the rare times in their histories, for their cultures have developed largely isolated from each other. When the Han Emperor Ming-ti encouraged Buddhist monks to bring their faith to China (64 A.D.), the secularistic-minded Chinese sought the religious comfort of an afterlife in the Buddha's promise of deliverance to Nirvana — something Chinese philosophies had left void. The Chinese sent streams of devout Buddhist pilgrims to India's monasteries and to seats of learning like Nalanda for centuries afterward. Such an enthusiast as the Chinese pilgrim, Fa-hsien, regarded India as the "Holy Land of Buddhism." During the years 399-414 he traveled, seeking the authentic texts of the *Vinaya-pitaka* or Buddhist books on monastic discipline. His journal, one of the authentic sources of the period, described the Gupta as an empire religiously tolerant, peaceful, prosperous, and well-governed.

The known world justifiably envied the achievements of the Gupta, which granted northern India political unity and peace for almost two centuries. But decline set in as the covetous eyes of central Asian barbarians awaited the decay of unified power. The Huns' attack in 455, although repulsed, so enervated Guptan armies that the empire virtually collapsed in 480. Two hundred years later, the Islamic tidal wave found northern India practically defenseless and an inviting political vacuum long after the splendor of Guptan culture had passed into history.

• Linguistic Unity and Diversity

Sanskrit, the language of the Aryans, served as did Latin in the West as the *lingua franca* for most of South Asia (meaning India, Pakistan, Bengla Desh and Ceylon). There were times when other languages challenged the supremacy of Sanskrit, as in the case of the Buddhist period when Pali became the language of the learned; but usually Sanskrit was the medium used for the exchange of ideas and culture. This is particularly true in north India where most of the languages prevalent today are derivatives of Sanskrit. Even Urdu, a language written in a Persian script, is not very different from Hindi, the modern tongue most directly akin to Sanskrit. Hindi is written in the Devangri (Sanskrit) script, but when spoken the difference between it and Urdu is minimal. One who speaks

Urdu can clearly understand one who speaks Hindi, though they may not be able to correspond in writing with one another.

Most of the citizenry of South Asian nations have been multilingual historically, especially the learned. The Aryan conquest established the supremacy of Sanskrit among the rulers by *ca.* 1000 B.C. The Muslims who conquered most of South Asia in the late medieval period (*ca.* 1200 to 1500 A.D.) favored Persian or Urdu, and much of the populace learned it. This was also true during the British era, though the English language was restricted to a much smaller number. Far less than one-half of 1 percent in India lay claim to English as their mother tongue, while fully 5 percent claim Urdu. The Aryan conquest also created a bloc of Sanskritized languages in North India. There are nearly a dozen languages derived from Sanskrit that are today spoken as mother tongues by over two-thirds of the population. An even greater percentage understands what is termed Hindustani, a *bazaar* language understood perhaps by 80 per cent or more of the populace.

Sanskrit was the dominant force as much because of culture as conquest. Sanskrit was the language of the Brahmins, the Aryan priests. Through the Brahmins a Sanskritized culture was imposed in most of South Asia. When in the post-classical period (600-1200 A.D.) Hindu culture emerged as the dominant socio-religious ethic, Sanskrit became a pan-South Asian tongue together with the Hindu life-style. As the so-called "great tradition" of Hinduism spread, it made accommodations for "small" or regional traditions and Sanskritized all of the north and most of the south of the subcontinent. Most of the region south of the Vindhya range resisted the linguistic expansion of the Aryans but accepted their cultural legacy. Thus the major Dravidian tongues of the south continued to flourish. Tamil, Telegu, and Kannada (the major Dravidian tongues) served as the base for regional identifications and expanded their literary output; but all incorporated Aryan concepts, ideals, and words into the indigenous outpourings.

• Hinduism: The Religion of Most of the People

Well over 80 percent of the population of India is and has been Hindu from the seventh century A.D. Hinduism resembles more a confederation of religions than it does a single, integrated cult. It is thus not like Christianity or Islam, which were puritanical and tightly organized. Hinduism, a tolerant faith. encompasses a wide range of beliefs that seem to many to be virtually contradictory. The diversity that exists in Hindu society as a whole understandably exists in the religion as a whole. Thus one can find philosophical justification and religious sanction for almost any ethical norm or structure. Few Westerners have been able to view Hinduism as a historical religion with a pattern of continuity and change not so different from other universal religions.

The scriptural bases of Hinduism are to be found in the *Vedas*, a collection of literature passed on from the Aryan tribes of antiquity. The Vedas are four in number, and many devout Hindus consider them to be the final authority. But Vedic literature was developed to meet the needs of a nomadic society; and much of the Vedas, particularly the *Rig Veda,* was probably composed outside of India itself. As the Aryans developed a more settled existence on the plains of north India, a new body of literature, which was primarily antithetical to the Vedas, was developed. The most famous and perhaps most significant of the new literature, the *Upanishads* (dialogues between the teachers and the taught), represented a reaction against Brahmanical ritualism and blind orthodoxy.

The bulk of the *Upanishads* was composed between 900-600 B.C. They are deep probings in dialogue form into questions of unity and diversity, reality and illusion, self and nature. Contrary to the teaching of Brahmins, the *Upanishads* repudiated sacrifice, magic, and mechanical rituals as paths to salvation. The most important idea to come out of the *Upanishads* perhaps was that *Atma* or self was identical with *Brahma* or the ultimate nature of reality. The philosophy of the *Upanishads* has been called *monism* because of its non-theistic view of overriding unity.

After the Aryans conquered North India (*ca.* 1500 B.C.), there slowly evolved a settled civilization centering on the Gangetic Plains, and the distinction between the conquering Aryans and the defeated *dasyu* slowly diminished. As they became less nomadic, the Aryans came to call the region Aryavarta (land of the Aryans). Pataliputra (modern day Patna) in the eastern Gangetic region evolved as the center of this new civilization. It was in this new civilization in the ancient state of Magadha that Buddha emerged and preached his anti-Brahmanical ideology of salvation. Buddhism, with its stress on non-violence (*ahimsa*) and ethical strengthening, became the moral basis of the Maurya universal state under Asoka (third century B.C.).

• The Varna System

The Aryans, long after their conquest, appear to have retained a feeling of racial superiority in regard to the conquered *dasyu* or dark-skinned. The fair-skinned victors devised elaborate rationales and rituals to keep their subjects in place. One of these rationales came to be termed the Varna System. *Varna* literally meant color, and it is quite possible that color was the decisive criterion used, at least in the beginning, in deciding where one should be placed on the social scale. But whatever the original purpose, it appears to have been lost sometime in the Buddhist Age, for the Buddhists revolted against the rigidity and exclusiveness of the Brahmins. What did remain to become peculiarly Indian was an idealized, socio-religious structure which argued that society (or those that count in it) was divided into four *varnas* or groups.

The four varna groupings in descending order of their importance came to be Brahmin (priests), Kshatriya (warriors and administrators), Vaishya (cultivators and merchants), and Sudra (peasants and menial laborers). The *dasyu* were, however, mostly outside the pale of what came to be Aryan society. A proletariat outside this pale came to be termed untouchable. Thus ancient India, as other classical civilizations, developed a system of stratification on the basis of function. The varna structure grew more rigid over the centuries, and by the Gupta period elaborate ceremonies and legal codes were developed to insure that the Sudra and the untouchables would never challenge the authority of the Brahmin or others higher on the social ladder. The famous Law Code of Manu, which dates from 2,000 years ago but probably altered later on, prescribed that those of low origin who heard the sacred teachings being discussed should have their tongues cut out and their ears filled with molten wax so as to insure they would neither repeat what they had heard nor listen again to that which they might pollute.

Dharma, or duty, virtue, law, was the core concept of the social system. A number of *dharmas* were developed in ancient legal texts (*smritis*) as modes of conduct for rulers, soldiers, priests, merchants, or cultivators. Each code contained guidelines for achieving the ultimate good within a given occupational group. Thus *rajdharma,* or king's code, offered guidance on how to govern most effectively. *Dharma* encouraged mobility and perfection within one's occupational grouping but discouraged mobility between the groups. It was believed that social corruption would occur when kings became merchants or when intellectuals became politicians or soldiers. The ideal was to become the best possible priest, politician, merchant or cultivator and accept the ranking within the system.

• The Jati System

Though the origins of the *jati* system are obscure, they appear to be clearly tied to more settled times than are associated with early Aryan society. The *jati* system probably did not develop fully until the era of the Gupta. During the Gupta period the jati evolved possibly from hereditary guilds or organizations based on a specialization of labor associated with a settled economy. There is little doubt that labor specialization played a significant role in jati formations, but over the centuries many jatis changed their specialties while members did not change their jati. Thus in the contemporary period it is not uncommon to find all the barbers of one area belonging to the same jati, while still another jati in a nearby city may be tied together by nothing more than kinship. Jati then can be defined either as extended kinship groupings or as groups that now share or at some time in the past appear to have shared job specialty. However, jati cannot easily be termed what it often has been termed, subcaste. Jati was apparently never a workable subdivision of varna, even though there are well over 3,000 different jati in India, and the tendency to classify the larger number as divisions of the fourfold varna classifications has proved nearly irresistible.

The jati, far more than the varna, has served as India's basic societal unit. The strong pollution prohibitions such as those associated with inter-marriage and inter-dining are tied primarily to jati. So also is pollution tied to job specialization. Untouchables who remove night soil or the dead carcasses of animals are considered highly polluted because of the nature of their work. Yet many untouchables have never undertaken unclean work; they are polluted because of lineage. The rules which govern the daily behavior of most Indians are set by the jati. One jati will not eat meat; others will, while still others will eat fish but not fowl. There exist fish-eating Brahmins along with Brahmins who will never consume anything not vegetarian. Untouchables in some areas of India have been considered so polluting that they have been required to remain far distant from others and have had to make loud noises when approaching people of higher station, while untouchables living in a different region have never experienced such treatment.

Each jati usually has a group of elders who regulate the behavior of its members, and these elders often exercise their prerogatives by ostracizing those who refuse to abide by the rules. Many Indians live in fear of being "outcaste," especially those who inhabit the rural areas. Being an outcaste means being denied the right of dining or marrying with one's own, and it can even be extended to one's family and siblings. Thus the importance of the jati as the societal unit which most claims the loyalty of a Hindu can easily be understood. It is this kinship group which has been the policing agent for the average Hindu for all of the modern era. Bold indeed has been the individual who challenged the elders of his jati.

Sun Temple Konark, Orissa State. Government of India Tourist Office, Chicago.

Every jati has its own *dharma* that its members are expected to follow, and this is what contributes greatly to India's diversity. Since there are over 3,000 jatis, there are well over 3,000 different sets of rules, or dharma. Also there exists more than one dharma. For everyone there is a general Hindu dharma as there is a general Christian ethic. The general dharma argues, for instance, that one should not eat beef, and the overwhelming majority do not. But here the similarity with Christianity ends, for Hindu dharma is also a philosophical abstraction that argues that each group has its own rights, duties, and responsibilities, even though many of these are absolutely contradictory to others. Thus one jati may require its members to be vegetarian, to abstain from taking life, and never to cross the ocean, while another jati may encourage the opposite. It has, therefore, proved difficult for governments to encourage similar actions on the part of its citizens when society not only condones but encourages each unit of the jati system to follow its own dharma.

Since the jati has been a basic unit in society from the Hindu Middle Ages through the eighteenth century, it is the unit to which many other socio-religious concepts are tied. An orthodox Hindu believes that his quest for immortality centers on his realizing the true nature of the relationship between brahman (universal soul) and atman (the individual's soul). He feels if he follows his dharma he will build up pure *karma* (result of action), and he will be reincarnated at a higher plane of existence. The orthodox Hindu views hell as existing here on earth and hopes to escape *samsara* (the cycle of rebirths) by doing what is correct, or following his dharma. If a Hindu builds up enough good karma, he will eventually reach *moksha* (release from rebirths), and the atman will be reunited with the universal creative essence, brahman. Rebirth to the Hindu is punishment, for it condemns him to repeat an earthly existence, either as man or beast, fish or fowl, and so on, as the atman migrates from one existence to another based on past karma. Every existence is based on a former life. Thus an untouchable who led a poor life in an earlier existence is simply being punished for past action (karma). The only way an untouchable can improve his position is through the practice of correct dharma and rebirth.

We must not overemphasize the orthodox ideal of Hinduism because modern Hinduism has changed as much as Christianity, Islam, or Buddhism. It would be as absurd to depict the modern West in terms of orthodox Christianity as it would to depict modern India in terms of orthodox Hinduism. It is thus important that these comments on the ideal of the Hindu tradition be weighed against later references in this text to social change in modern India.

• The Islamic Community: A Vocal Minority

Today 12 percent of India is Muslim. Prior to the 1947 separation of India and Pakistan the percentage was around 25 percent. Thus the role of Islam in the subcontinent and in the Republic of India has historically been larger than the 12 percent might otherwise indicate. And though Muslims, as the followers of the prophet Muhammad term themselves, are late-comers to civilization in India, their role in India has been significant and their contribution large. Muhammad (570-632) is the inspiration for Muslim thought and culture; and the *Quran* (Koran), a book completed shortly after his death, is the source of all authority according to his followers. For centuries observers have admired the success of Islam and attributed it to the simplicity of its doctrine or the success of its arms.

Many have viewed it as a medieval storm that overwhelmed most opposition in its attempt at world dominion. Others have marveled at the strength of the Islamic organization which swept out of the Arabian desert, united by the creed: "There is but one God, Allah, and Muhammad is his prophet." Others still have viewed Islam as a retarding or intolerant ethic, for a fear and distrust of Islam has been long ingrained in the minds of men, Hindu and Christian as well as Hebrew. Such explanations do, however, seem quite insufficient.

Islam was born at the crossroads of empire. Within easy reach of Arabia are to be found most of the regions which gave birth to the ancient civilizations of the world. Nearby are the lands where Christ first lectured to his disciples, where the Jews came to know captivity, where the Pharaohs sat amid theocratic splendor, and where for centuries the Zoroastrian Persians, the Hellenistic Greeks, and the conquering Romans mingled ideals and concepts. The spread of Islam in such an area was perhaps inevitable, and it seems ridiculous to explain its spread as a result of its being a simple religion born in desert wastes among people of a militant and aggressive tradition. Southwest Asia was anything but primitive at the time of the rise and triumph of Islam. Other reasons account for the fact that every seventh person in the world today is Muslim. Perhaps the explanation lies in doctrine.

In many respects Islam resembles other religions. It is monotheistic and shares much of the cosmology of the Judeo-Christian tradition. It claims Muhammad as the last or "seal" of the prophets but respects most of the important figures in the Judeo-Christian tradition. It does not accept Christ as God but as a prophet. Likewise, Muhammad is a prophet, not a god. Members of the faith should not be called Muhammadans, for he is not worshipped by followers of Islam. The correct name is Muslim or Moslem. A Muslim (one who submits to Allah) distrusts those who, he feels, do not practice monotheism, including those who believe in the Christian trinity, which is held to be a belief in polytheism. Also strong is the conviction that idolatry is evil and that human representations ought not to grace the *masjid* (mosque or building of worship).

Islam favors charity, particularly toward those within the Islamic brotherhood, and frowns on usury. It asks its adherents not to wrong others and promises that they, in turn, will not be wronged. It argues that "Allah Knows All Things" and that contracts, particularly those written, should not be broken. What then has made Islam unique? Why have Europe and South Asia opposed it? Perhaps simply because it borders each area, politically and culturally, now and in the past. Still, there seem to be other reasons. Both the Hindu and the Christian have reacted bitterly to the Muslim concept of *jihad* (holy war), which promises salvation to all who die on the battlefield attempting to spread Islam to the non-believers. Muslims on the other hand find it difficult to understand why nonbelievers condemn the jihad, for to them a jihad is simply a group of believers attempting to carry out the will of God.

Muslims also fail to comprehend why the application of *jizya* has elicited violent response from non-Muslims, especially in India. Jizya is a tax imposed on non-Muslims when the government is dominated by Muslims. Islam holds that the world is composed of two spheres, the abode of peace and that of war. The peaceful sphere is the area over which Islam presides. A non-believer may live within this sphere, especially if he belongs to a tradition which has a holy book, so long as he pays tax for the privilege. Muslims feel that they are tolerant when they permit non-believers to exist within a Muslim state and that non-believers should pay for the privilege. The jizya next to the jihad has been the most hotly contested issue in India historically. Those Muslim leaders termed great by the Hindu majority are those like Akbar, a Mughal (also, Mogul) ruler of the late sixteenth century, who chose not to implement the tax. Other rulers like the Emperor Aurangzeb (1658-1707) helped bring on war by imposing it and in the process destroyed Islamic paramountcy in India and opened the doors for British penetration. Aurangzeb to a Hindu was a great bigot, but to a Muslim he was a religious zealot, implementing only what was expected of him.

Many differences between Muslims and Hindus that exist on the popular level often lead to mutual antagonism. Muslims eat beef; Hindus do not. Muslims do not eat pork; Hindus are permitted to do so. Muslims have no special priestly class, unlike the Hindus. Muslims worship together on Friday while the Hindus have no special day for prayer. Islam forbids dancing and music during worship while Hinduism encourages the use of music. Islam disparages visual depictions of God; Hinduism relishes them as much as any religion on the globe. Muslims pray publicly five times daily; Hindus usually limit their daily devotion to a private room. A Muslim is expected, if possible, to make a pilgrimage to Mecca; the Hindu makes his pilgrimage to holy places within India. The Hindu (at least philosophically) admires asceticism; the Muslim does not. Only during Ramadan, when Muslims are expected not to partake of food or drink from sunrise to sundown for one month, do they even come close to an ascetic tradition. And finally the Muslim abhors the jati or caste system, while the Hindu sees little to admire in the Muslim promise of equality within the brotherhood of Islam because the provision is tied to a religious exclusiveness that postulates one path to salvation.

• Islamic Conquest

In the early eighth century, the first wave of Islamic expansion carried Muslim banners across North Africa to Europe. India, on the opposite flank of Islam, was virtually ignored, though an Arabian general in 711 entered the Indus Valley. Islam did not appear in South Asia in force until a second wave of conquest carried Islamic culture to Central Asia and Afghanistan. Islam did penetrate many of the port cities along India's west coast, but Muslim merchants in these settlements seem to have created no challenge to Hindu hegemony, and peaceful trade relations developed between the Arab and Indian worlds. The mutual antagonism, hatred, and hostility that have come to characterize Hindu-Muslim relations in the last millenium seem to be a direct result of the assaults on the Hindu world launched by Central Asian peoples who had been themselves converted to Islam only shortly before. The first and perhaps most famous of these intruders was Mahmud of Ghazni. Between 1000 and 1026 A.D., from his fortress city of Ghazni, he led about twenty expeditions down from the mountain citadel. Mahmud carried back to the hills of Afghanistan great wealth that had been looted from Hindu homes and temples; and waves of Turks, Afghans, Mongols, and other peoples followed his lead in the centuries that followed.

The Hindus who inhabited the plains seemed incapable of sustaining a system of united defense, and around 1200 the Muslims succeeded in establishing a Muslim state in north India known as the Delhi Sultanate. Sultan literally means "one who wields authority," authority bestowed by the Caliph, the theocratic head of the Islamic state and successor of the Prophet Muhammad. From 1206 to 1526 the Delhi sultans, supposedly as the agents of Caliphs, spread religious tyranny among all the peoples of South Asia. Hindu temples were destroyed, Buddhist monasteries were looted, and icons and statues were defaced with impunity. The Sultans looked upon India as a region where jihad should be applied, and for centuries the fury of the Muslim zealots knew few bounds. Also the Muslim hierarchy, which distrusted the indigenous, reinforced its position by importing foreigners from Central Asia, mostly slaves. There slaves were castrated as young boys and raised to be rulers. Eunuchs, it was felt, would give all their loyalty to the conquering minority, not to family, and so the thirteenth century is usually termed the era of the Slave or Eunuch Kings. The slave system could not endure, and in the early fourteenth century Muhammad bin Tughluq succeeded in establishing a state which encompassed the largest amount of territory ruled by any dynasty since the reign of Asoka in the third century B.C. Muhammad Tughluq was a ferocious ruler. He made an art of torture, and the Tughluq state did not long survive his death in 1351, for by 1400 the Tughluq Sultanate had ceased to be an important kingdom. Regional rulers appeared who resisted the attempts of various succeeding Sultans to return the unity of the past. And as decline set in, Delhi rulers lost contact with the Afghan areas which had provided the manpower and stimulus necessary for conquest some centuries earlier. Contact was, however, re-established forcefully in 1526 by Babar, a Mongol king from Kabul, Afghanistan, who again swept onto the Indian plains to found a new dynasty in the Delhi area.

• The Mughal Dynasty

Babar defeated the last of the Sultans near Delhi on the plains of Panipat and thus established the Mughal Dynasty. Mughal is a corruption of Mongol, for Babar was a Mongol who traced his lineage to Genghis Khan and the famous Timur, who on a destructive foray in 1398-99 dealt a blow to the Delhi Sultanate from which it never recovered. Babar actually claimed he had the right to rule in Delhi based on Timur's conquest, though he preferred to reside in Kabul. Babar disliked the Indian plains, and he remained with his courts in the mountains most of the time; but he followed an enlightened policy in regard to his Hindu subjects, and most of the forced conversions and bloody destruction of the Sultanate era ceased. Akbar, his grandson, who ruled India from 1556-1605, followed the lead of his famous ancestor, and from 1556 till 1605 relations between the Muslim and the Hindu improved rapidly.

Traditional India reached its zenith under the Mughal administration. Four able men whose reigns span the period, 1556-1707, provided the stability necessary for the Indian subcontinent to flourish as it never has since. Akbar, the first of the great Mughals, provided good government and unity, in part, through an enlightened religious policy. Akbar had all the land of the realm surveyed and developed a tax and legal structure, much of which survived into the twentieth century. Akbar also fostered the arts and encouraged religious debate to be held publicly at his court in Fatehpur Sikri, his capital that still stands near the modern city of Agra as a silent testament to the skill of the artisans who built it centuries ago. The successors of Akbar were also builders, and South Asia from Agra to Lahore is full of monuments which testify to the magnificence of the era. The son and successor of Akbar, Jahangir (1605-27), continued his father's policy of building monumental structures, but it was under Shah Jahan (1628-58) that Mughal construction reached its fulfillment. Shah Jahan virtually bankrupted the nation with his extensive building program. The

The Taj Mahal in Agra. Government of India Tourist Office, Chicago.

Taj Mahal, which he built as a final resting place for his favorite wife, Mumtaz Mahal, is considered to be the world's most beautiful building; but it was built at a tremendous cost. For nearly twenty years, seven days a week, over 20,000 workmen labored to build the colossal Taj. Aurangzeb (1659-1707), who was the last of the great Mughals, was more austere than his predecessors; and he, preferring to live in those buildings of his ancestors, built no monuments of note.

The empire so ably presided over by Akbar is thought by many historians to have been the best-managed state of its day. Akbar was a tolerant ruler and an able administrator. He took as brides two Rajput princesses, and these marriages to Hindu females of high-caste ranking helped quiet opposition and insure loyalty, especially among the militant Rajputs. But it was his repeal of the jizya, which the Hindu viewed as a symbol of second-class citizenship, that endeared him to Hindus for all time and helped encourage peace and prosperity throughout the kingdom. Without the able rule of Akbar, it is to be doubted if his successors, Jahangir and Shah Jahan, would ever have been able to build the colossal structures for which they are justly famous. It is perhaps also to be regretted that Shah Jahan, builder of the exquisite Taj Mahal, was the man who reinstituted a policy of destruction in regard to Hindu temples. It was this policy coupled with that of Aurangzeb, his son and successor, that caused India once again to erupt into war. Aurangzeb not only destroyed temples; he brought back the jizya. The result was war on a scale not seen in centuries. A Hindu leader named Shivaji rallied his people, the Marathas, and challenged the Mughals at every turn. Before long the Maratha people were the power in much of the subcontinent, and the once proud Mughals saw their empire quickly eclipsed. Even before Aurangzeb died while fighting the Marathas in 1707, it was clear that his policy had failed. He had weakened the state beyond repair.

• Other Religious Minorities

Next to the Hindu and Muslim communities today, as in the past, all others are insignificant numerically. About 2.5 percent of the population of the Republic of India is Christian, .5 percent is Jain, nearly 2 percent is Sikh, and less than half of 1 percent are Parsi. Christians are congregated primarily in the state of Kerala, a province that appears to have been Christian for 1500 years or more. The Kerala Christians, also known as Syrian Christians, claim that the apostle Thomas brought the word of Christ to India and that he is buried there. Until the early nineteenth century there were few other Christians in India, except the Roman Catholics who inhabited enclaves like Portuguese Goa or French Pondicherry. British administrators reluctantly opened India to Christian proselytism in 1813, and, though missionary activity increased rapidly, the number of converts was never large.

The Jains are another minority that has never enjoyed a large following, though they date their founding to the time of the Buddha or earlier. But again their numbers are not indicative of their legacy historically. The Jain concern for life strongly affected Buddhist and Hindu thought. The Jains are famous in India for their contribution of *ahimsa,* an ancient doctrine later borrowed by Hindus and Buddhists, which is usually explained as meaning non-injury to all living things. It is not uncommon to see a Jain wear what looks like a surgical mask in order that no living thing should enter his mouth; sometimes they also are seen with feather dusters which they use to sweep the path before them as they walk.

The Jains are, however, not the smallest important minority; the 200,000 Parsi claim that distinction. The Parsis, like the Jains, are important in the mercantile realm, and they exert influence far beyond their numbers. The Parsi community claims to be Zoroastrian or Persian in origin and to have migrated to India around the eighth century in order to escape Muslim expansion in West Asia. They have always gotten on well with the Europeans, in part because they closely resemble each other, and this helps explain their importance as a community in recent centuries.

The last significant minority group is the Sikh. Sikhism is an eclectic religion which has borrowed heavily from Hindu and Muslim thought. Though Sikhs are today identified as militant, they were initially a very pacifistic community. The religion dates to early Mughal years and particularly to Guru Nanak (1469-1539), the founder, whose followers called themselves Sikhs (disciples). Nine spiritual leaders called Guru (teacher) followed Nanak, and it was the Ten Gurus collectively that formalized the religion. The Punjab is the province where most Sikhs reside, though they have spread over most of North India. Sometimes their distinct appearance gives the impression that Sikhs number more than they do, for they stand out wherever they appear. Because of the persecution and even execution of Gurus by Mughal Emperors after Akbar, a Sikh Khalsa (pure fraternity), distinct in appearance, appeared. Govind Singh, the Tenth Guru, required that all Sikhs wear a particular type of undergarment, wear a steel bracelet, carry a dagger or sword, carry a comb, and never cut their hair. The long hair has necessitated the wearing of a turban over the long, tightly-wrapped hair. Also all Sikhs have as their last name Singh (lion). The five requirements, or five K's as they are called, helped develop a distinctive character among Sikhs as well as helping to turn them into a militant community. The last Guru, Govind Singh, was horrified by the decapitation of his predecessor by Aurangzeb, and he turned the Sikhs away from pacificism in self-defense.

• India: Rural and Urban

Many people like to speak of two Indias — one urban and sophisticated, the other rural and technologically backward. There is no doubt that many nations have this type of gulf, but it is equally true that the gulf seems greater in India. A large part of rural India, particularly in the northeast, is peopled by tribal aboriginals who have always lived outside the pale of Hindu society. One of these groups, the Nagas, have given up head-hunting in this century. Most of rural India is, however, not aboriginal or animistic; most of it is Hindu and Muslim. Most of it is also poor and has been so for centuries. Technology did not begin to penetrate the traditional countryside until recently, and poverty and hunger have long marred life in the rural areas. This is partly due to the startling increase in population during the last century. Economic development under the British was slow, but the population grew rapidly. The disparity in incomes between the rural and urban people seemed to grow in proportion to the length of British rule. In the eighteenth century the British conquered a relatively prosperous South Asia; in 1947 they left it a torn, tattered, poor, and overpopulated land. While British rule was on the whole humane, the colonial exploitation helped destroy rural India. British industrial products flooded the hinterlands and destroyed the livelihood of many skilled artisans. Under the British, rural or traditional India paid the price for the development of the great urban centers built by the British — Calcutta, Madras, and Bombay.

While urban India grew (and perhaps flourished) under the British aegis, rural India remained tied to the weather and the ancient agricultural techniques. Rural India even to the present day is virtually dependent on the monsoon rains. If the rains fail, as they do from time to time, Indians starve. Because there has not been any exclusive production of agricultural products for many a decade, there are no granary stores to fall back on. India, which was a grain exporter until half a century ago, exists without a commodity surplus. And when the rains fall, as they did in 1966 and 1967, India with her teeming millions faces famine on a magnitude unknown in the Western world, partly because 80 percent of Indians live in rural areas, and the communication network essential to a famine relief program simply does not exist, at least not one capable of moving foodstuffs quickly and efficiently to millions of starving people.

2

The Making of British India

AS THEY COMMENCED their "Age of Exploration," which reflected the insufficiency of their homelands, Europeans first came to India to trade, not to conquer. To many of the early European adventurers, however, the difference between the two motives was small. The Portuguese, who arrived first in 1498, quickly succeeded in establishing fortified settlements at strategic locations around the coastlines of the Indian Ocean. The Portuguese never managed to get beyond these "enclaves," and their mercantile empire was built on the sea, not on the land. Mercantilism, the prevailing economic practice, sought to accumulate gold and silver by an excess of exports over imports. Portugal in the sixteenth century was a small nation and lacked the manpower necessary for territorial expansion. The Portuguese, however, constructed a prosperous "enclave system" based on fortified settlements at Goa, Ormuz, Diu, Malacca, and later Macao in the South China Sea. Each enclave was under the charge of a factor, and the collection of buildings used for trade and fabrication within was termed a factory. Thus the system was based on the factory or trading post rather than on land acquisition.

The Portuguese based their "empire" on the silk, spice, and luxury trade which was highly lucrative. The Venetian city-states and the Arabs had long prospered because of their roles as middlemen in the trade between Europe and Asia. The Portuguese ended this monopoly, and the center of East-West trade began to shift to the Atlantic periphery of Europe and away from the Adriatic and Mediterrenean. Spices, silks, and luxury items such as jewels, porcelain, and artisanware flowed to Europe in Portuguese ships. Naturally, the Portuguese were looked upon with envy by merchants who also enjoyed a favorable location on Europe's western seaboard, and before long their ships came to be common sights in the Indian Ocean.

● The Trading Companies

Unfortunately for the Portuguese merchants, just at the time when the Dutch and British merchants were aggressively moving to challenge them, domestic affairs of the Iberian Peninsula seriously curtailed Portugal's ability to meet the challenges posed by her European neighbors. When the Portuguese throne fell vacant in 1580, Philip II of Spain forcibly united the Iberian Peninsula by annexing Portugal. Philip then proceeded to ignore the needs of Portuguese merchants, particularly if they conflicted with those of Spain. The obvious sentiment of the ruling house encouraged another part of the Spanish Empire to attempt to destroy the monopoly enjoyed by the Portuguese in Asian seas throughout the sixteenth century. The Low Countries, as that portion of the Spanish Empire dominated by Dutch mercantile interest was then termed, had long been attempting to share in the profits of Eastern trade. Dutch ships completed their first round trip via the Cape of Good Hope in 1597. It took them that long to overcome Philip's adamant refusal to grant the Dutch permission to use Iberian ports and to obtain from the Catholic Iberians the maps and knowledge necessary to get there. Following the first success, Dutch merchants outfitted many more ships and in 1602 founded the famous Dutch East India Company in order to better facilitate trade.

The Dutch, however, were never really involved in India, but for a short time their interest in South Asia focused on Ceylon. Though they did not entirely confine their trade to Indonesia, they centered it there after nearly eliminating Portuguese influence in Southeast Asia with the capture of Malacca in 1641. Britain, a working partner of the Dutch, replaced the Portuguese as the European power in India. The British, throughout the period from 1560 to 1660, sided with the Dutch because of mutual antagonism toward Catholic Spain. When Portugal was annexed in 1580, both the Dutch and the British took advantage of the forced unity to destroy the Portuguese in the East. A series of religious wars in Holland, which saw Spanish troops decimate the Protestant population, resulted in open reprisals and warfare on the high seas against the Portuguese, who were viewed by all but the Portuguese themselves as citizens of Philip II of Spain.

The British were actually the last Europeans to enter Asian trade in force because of preoccupation with their American empire between 1620-1780. Also the British had many religious questions and a civil war to settle at home. But as the 1600s came to a close and the religious problems seemed to fade, the British, who had chartered the British East India Company in 1600, now began to push a more active trade policy in India. Britain's Revolution of 1688 witnessed the triumph of influential commercial interests in Parliament over certain political prerogatives of the crown. The new policy coincided with the loss of vitality on the part of the Mughal Empire under the Emperor Aurangzeb. The long war in India brought on by Aurangzeb's policy left the Mughal dynasty prostrate by the time of his death in 1707.

• Anglo-French Rivalry

The power vacuum created by a dying Mughal regime invited others to vie for supremacy. For twenty-five years most of the attempts to replace the mighty Mughals centered on the indigenous Marathas or on the Afghans who had again begun to pressure Delhi. But this changed in the 1740s when Joseph Dupleix, the Governor of Pondicherry, began to commit European soldiers to fight in the interior of South India. Dupleix was employed by the French East India Company, an organization which never played a significant role in Indian affairs directly. Dupleix, however, did have an enormous impact. He learned early that the fragmentation of the Mughal state made it easy to apply the European "balance of power" policy to India. He would provide well-trained Europeans, who possessed superior fire power, to the various princely claimants in the Karnatic, the plains between Madras and the Deccan Plateau. When a prince whom he supported emerged victorious, he would then make known the demands of the French Government, the owners of the French Company. The British, noting how successful the policy was, rapidly followed suit. Robert Clive, an employee of the British East India Company in Madras, rallied British Company loyalists and routed the French, climaxing the Anglo-French "World War," which encompassed the American French and Indian War and Europe's Seven Years' War. Dupleix was recalled in disgrace, and Clive came to be regarded as one of the founders of British India.

• British Conquest

Anglo-French machinations frightened Indian leaders. Siraj-ud-daula, the Nawab or Governor of Bengal, decided to end foreign intervention in territory under his jurisdiction. The Nawab was, in theory, the underling of the Great Mughal in Delhi. But since the death of Aurangzeb in 1707, governors had virtually ignored the Great Mughal and had acted like independent sovereigns. Acting hastily, he ordered the British to leave Calcutta, one of their three major bases in India. When the British refused to leave, the Nawab had them arrested and interred in a small cell that came to be known to the world as the "Black Hole of Calcutta," because nearly all of those imprisoned allegedly smothered to death within hours. Though many doubt the Black Hole story, there is no doubt that the Nawab's actions again brought Clive back into the picture. Clive moved from Madras and quickly chastised the Nawab in 1757 at the Battle of Plassey, a contest won more through cunning than through weaponry. Clive bribed supposed supporters of the Nawab not to fight for the Indian during the battle. However, Plassey proved inconclusive, for local princes were not yet ready to concede defeat. Another round seemed inevitable. Clive, who had been resting on his laurels in Britain, returned to India. In 1764, while Clive was en route, British arms at Buxar decisively defeated the Nawab of Oudh, the governor of the territory adjacent to Bengal. When Clive arrived in 1765, the British had only to decide where the borders of their new-found empire should be drawn. Nothing lay ahead of them in North India for a thousand miles except the vast Gangetic Plains and a Mughal Emperor in Delhi whose day had long since passed. Clive chose to accept this defeated monarch as his political superior and in 1765 had the East India Company appointed by the Great Mughal to the office of Diwan (revenue collector) of Bengal, Bihar, and Orissa. This agreement had two consequences: it kept the Mughal Emperor alive as a legal fiction, and the British East India Company became a functionary of the Great Mughal, making its legality beyond question, or so the Company argued.

• Consolidation of Company Rule

Merchants founded the British Raj (rule) in India, but it was the bureaucrats who ruled India during most of the British period. The transition from Company to Crown rule was not simple, nor was it carried out as expeditiously as it might have been. The British East India Company claimed the right to rule until 1858, as did the Great Mughal, for whom it continued, supposedly, to administer. Parliament was not happy about the peculiar system that had been devised by Clive and others, but it was reluctant to end the Company's prerogatives through the legislative process. While it was true that the Crown helped the Company establish suzerainty in India, it was equally true that conquest was primarily a result of Company policy, funding, personnel, and arms. Parliament was reluctant to claim what others had built.

Following the victory at Buxar, British merchants expanded their sway through a series of wars and agreements concluded in India with local princes, as often as not against the expressed desires of the directors of the Company in London. In the process many "servants" of the Company amassed enormous wealth, including Robert Clive, while the Company in whose name all lands were conquered was threatened with bankruptcy. Criticism of Company servants grew, as did the demand for control of Company activities. When Clive returned to Britain, he was faced with a parliamentary inquiry into the sources of his wealth. Though cleared, he committed suicide in 1774. Clive's successor, Warren Hastings, fared little better; he was recalled from India in disgrace and brought before the House of Lords for a great public trial that lasted six years. Though Hastings was acquitted, the British government gained the ascendancy. Parliament asserted its right to supervise the Company it had chartered.

Actually Hastings himself represented the first real attempt to control the Company. He was appointed Governor-General in 1774 as a result of provisions imposed by the Regulating Act of 1773, an act prompted by the threatened bankruptcy of the Company. But because the 1773 Act was ambiguous in regard to the exercise of power in India, the Pitt India Act, which provided for joint Crown and Company participation or jurisdiction, was passed in 1784. By the terms of the Pitt Act suzerainty passed to a newly created Board of Control and out of the hands of the proprietors of the Company, who retained sole control over commercial transactions. The Board of Control was very much concerned about the image created by the trial of Hastings that through the late 1780s seemed as though it would never end. With attention focused on scandal and the need for reform, the Company's charter came up for renewal once more.

The charter renewal of 1793 started a tradition. Henceforth the Company received its renewal every twenty years; and every time the year for renewal grew near, the demand for change swept across Britain. Thus the charter renewals of 1813, 1833, and 1853 are important landmarks in Indian history. In 1813 the Company lost its monopoly of the Indian trade to the free trade advocates and was forced as well to open the doors of India to Christian missionaries. In 1833 the Company lost its commercial rights altogether and became simply the legal agent of the Crown, vested solely with the political administration of the land. In 1853 the Company lost control over patronage when open competition became mandatory for all appointed to the Indian Civil Service.

• The Cornwallis Legacy

As part of the plan to renovate the Company's image and administration, Lord Charles Cornwallis, who had commanded the British Army in the last decisive battle of the American Revolution, was appointed Governor-General of India. Cornwallis, who knew little or nothing about India, was considered a paragon of virtue, and his years, 1786-1793, were identified with reform — though strongly Anglicized. He consolidated the higher company offices into an organization subsequently known as the Indian Civil Service (the I.C.S.). Members of the I.C.S., in return for higher salaries, promised not to engage in trade nor to accept gifts. The major criticism of Company servants was thus muted, and men of questionable integrity or doubtful morality began to seek their fortunes elsewhere. The I.C.S. was proud of its high salary, its prestige, and its Anglicized character. The organization became known as the "Steel Framework," the structure which because of its loyal, honest, frugal, and intelligent membership held together the entire structure of British India. The I.C.S. was racist to its very core, and no apology was offered because of it; in fact, pride was its most distinguishing characteristic throughout its long existence.

Another perplexing problem that Cornwallis solved centered on what has often been termed the "search for the landlord." Cornwallis, like many of his British peers, felt someone must own the land. He did not seem to appreciate that the Mughal concept of a *Zamindar* (tax collector) differed from that of a landowner in the west. The Zamindar, because of meritorious service, was assigned land from which to collect taxes and as a reward kept a part of the taxes. The Mughal Emperor owned the land; the Zamindar was his steward. The difference in point of view was significant, for under the terms of the Permanent Settlement of 1793, Cornwallis settled the land on the Zamindars in return for fixed annual payments to the Company. Thus the Zamindars became owners or landlords at the expense of others, particularly the cultivators. It was a heavy price to pay for creating a landed nobility that might be loyal in perpetuity, for it resulted in the creation of a class of parasitic, absentee landlords that every Indian government ever since has attempted with little success to eliminate. The Permanent Settlement was recognized as a blunder almost immediately, and as the British Raj spread beyond Bengal, Bihar, and Orissa, land in other areas was often settled on the *raiyats* (peasant cultivators) rather than on the tax collectors.

As the eighteenth century drew to a close, the Company appeared to have worked out a system whereby many could prosper. Parliament was pleased by the Cornwallis policy; he had raised the image of the Company and, perhaps more important, had refused to continue the policy of aggressive and expensive expansion so disliked and feared by many in Britain. The Company as master of Bengal, Bihar, and Orissa already ruled an area with a population larger than that of Britain. But Lord Richard Wellesley Mornington, the Governor-General who arrived in 1797, had other ideas. He followed an aggressive expansionist policy for the next seven years under the guise of defense against a possible attack by Egyptian-based troops of Napoleon Bonaparte. Finally in 1805 he was recalled, but not before he had managed to involve the British in a series of wars with the Marathas. After a brief respite of nearly eight years (which the Company used to replenish its treasury), the Maratha resistance was crushed, and by 1818 the British were the paramount power on the subcontinent. From 1818 to 1947 the British ruled India with a firm hand and from a position of unquestioned military supremacy. Virtually hundreds of princely states remained outside British India, but all had to conclude subsidiary alliances which made them recognize British paramountcy and accept a resident European to serve as an "advisor."

• Westernizing of the Governmental Structure

Though some westernizing of the political and social structure occurred in the eighteenth century, it did not become policy until 1828, the year in which William Bentinck became Governor-General. The elder bureaucrats in the administration, known as the Orientalists, argued that the Company should conform when possible to Mughal ways. The Orientalists, many of whom helped found the empire in the subcontinent, were not all opposed to westernization or essential change; many simply feared it might lead to social demoralization and chaos, especially if change were directed at social and religious rather than political structures. It was one thing to set up a political superstructure; it was another to force alien-inspired social and religious ideas, values, and attitudes, as many of the younger bureaucrats, known as the Anglicists, planned. Also many Orientalists actually saw much to admire in India culturally and religiously, while the Anglicists saw little that was not reprehensible.

The Bentinck era (1828-1835), perhaps more than any other, came to be identified with the Anglicists. Though the European nature of the bureaucracy had always made it sensitive to demands for change emanating from London, this was a period when those demanding change were in the ascendancy. The Anglicists had grown in strength as the Company grew and by the 1830s were gaining support from new quarters.

In Britain, Evangelical reformers, foremost of whom was a group known as the Clapham Sect, agitated publicly for reform from the top by pressuring Parliament, while the Utilitarians, foremost of whom was Jeremy Bentham, attempted to institute reform from within the Company itself. Bentham taught at Haileybury, an institution set up by the Company to train young men for service in India, and his friend James Mill shared a similar influence within the Company, especially after the publication in 1817 of his monumental *History of India.* Bentinck, an avowed Utilitarian, and other Evangelicals like William Wilberforce felt they had a duty to help remake India, though their motives differed. The Utilitarians thought many Indian customs were based on useless and expensive traditions, not on utility, while the Evangelicals viewed Indians as heathens or idolators who needed to be reformed.

Under Bentinck the Anglicists had their way. Bentinck forbade the practice of *sati*, the immolation of widows on the funeral pyres of their husbands. He also launched an aggressive campaign against the *thugi*, groups of thieves and murderers who claimed such action was a part of their dharma or way of life. Similarly, infanticide was prohibited as were other practices long accepted by the Hindu but which Bentinck argued were counter to all moral and ethical systems. Bentinck and the Anglicists ran roughshod over the Orientalists, and they swelled their ranks as a result of the Charter Act of 1833. Under its terms Thomas Babington Macaulay, the famed essayist and historian, joined the Bentinck administration. Quickly, Macaulay became a driving force for westernization through education. Because of his influence and his position as Law Member on the Council of the Governor-General, Macaulay was given the opportunity to spread his often-quoted belief that the best way to educate or reform was by creating a class "Indian in blood and color, but English in taste, in opinions, in morals, and intellect." Macaulay, though he lacked facility in any South Asian tongue, argued in his famous "Minute" or Memorial to Bentinck in 1835 that he had "never found one among them [Indians] who could deny that a single shelf of a good European library was worth the whole native literature of India and Arabia."

Macaulay and Bentinck, like most of the Anglicist bureaucrats who followed in their steps, actually came to feel they knew what was best for India. They argued that India needed British ideals, institutions, and administrators. In 1835, English replaced Persian as the language of the courts, and before long future Indian barristers were flocking to the European schools where westernized education could be obtained. Even though westernization continued unabated, the pace was slower than many Anglicists had hoped. In part, this was because the new education

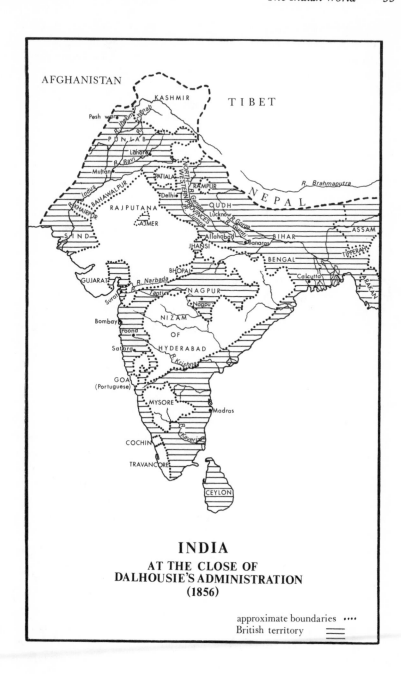

AFGHANISTAN

KASHMIR

TIBET

Pesh wara

PUNJAB

Lahore

R. Ravi

Multan

Indus

BAHAWALPUR

KHAIRPOR

RAJPUTANA

AJMER

SIND

PATIALA

RAMPUR

Delhi

NORTHERN
PROVINCES
WESTERN

R. Brahmaputra

NEPAL

OUDH

Lucknow

R. Ganges

R. Jumna

R. Gumti

Allahabad

Banaras

BIHAR

ASSAM

JHANSI

BENGAL

TIPPERAH

BHOPAL

GUJARAT

R. Narbada

Surat

Taptı

NAGPUR

Nagpur

Calcutta

ARAKAN

Bombay

Poona

NIZAM

OF

HYDERABAD

Satara

R. Krishna

GOA
(Portuguese)

MYSORE

Madras

COCHIN

R. Kaveri

TRAVANCORE

CEYLON

INDIA
AT THE CLOSE OF
DALHOUSIE'S ADMINISTRATION
(1856)

approximate boundaries ••••
British territory ═══

never got beyond the confines of the new group Macaulay had predicted would arise. English ideals did not "trickle down" to the masses; they remained the property of the select few who prepared for future roles in the administration, primarily as barristers.

• Company Relations with the Princely States

Bentinck and others encountered little Indian opposition to their enforced reforms, probably because of the peaceful nature of administrative efforts between 1818 and 1839. Only a fairly small and indecisive police effort in Burma in the 1820s disrupted the quiet consolidation of the British Raj in this period. Governors-General constantly interfered in the affairs of the princely states, usually through the "advisors" who had been forced on local rulers through some three hundred separate treaties. All of these treaties included recognition of the Company as the "paramount" power in the subcontinent. The claim of paramountcy enabled the British to appoint, recognize, and replace native rulers with impunity. Of course, the British always rationalized such involvement in the internal affairs of the "Native States" as actions necessary for the good of "their" people. Though over five hundred native states survived and remained outside British India, their independence was more nominal than real. The one real exception to this status in the first half of the nineteenth century was the Lahore-based state of Ranjit Singh. Singh ruled over an ably-administered state in the Punjab (land of the five rivers) until his death in 1839.

Many Europeans had long been interested in the Sikh state of Ranjit Singh because of its strategic importance. It was felt to be an area that would help round out the natural boundaries of the Company, for its territory included all the land in the northwest from the plains to the foothills of the great mountain ranges of the north. Lucrative trade also seemed possible, for the state sat astride the Indus and its major tributaries. Ranjit Singh had accepted a resident advisor as a result of a treaty negotiated in 1832, but he was able to resist further encroachments, primarily because the British respected his ability and that of his regular army of 75,000. The Sikh state was, however, too dependent on the personality of Singh, and his death in the summer of 1839 unleashed the forces of disruption and disintegration. Ranjit's son and successor was assassinated in 1840, as was his successor in 1843. Sikh factionalism threatened to bring total chaos, for no leader appeared with the charisma necessary to restore order. The invitation was more than Company officials could resist, and between 1845 and 1848 the Lahore state of

Ranjit Singh vanished as a result of military operations brought to conclusion under Lord Dalhousie, Governor-General from 1848 to 1856.

• The Dalhousie Years

Dalhousie annexed not only the Punjab; he actually made Britain master of India from Burma to Afghanistan. Dalhousie could rightly claim to be the ruler of India, and in 1852 he added lower Burma to the Company's domains. In fact, the only area which the Company wanted to add to its territory in the period 1839-1857 which eluded its grasp was Afghanistan. They tried in the first Afghan War of 1839-42, but they failed miserably in 1842 when their invading army of nearly 16,000 was annihilated to a man by either the weather or the ferocity of Afghan warriors. Dalhousie's success in the Punjab seemed to increase his hostility towards all that was Indian, and he pushed westernization there, imposing new civil and criminal codes and undertaking large public projects in road building and irrigation, which eventually made the Punjab one of the most prosperous provinces of British India. A testament to the success of Dalhousie in the Punjab occurred in 1857 when the Sikhs remained loyal to their British overlords while most of the rest of north India rose in armed rebellion, mostly as a result of the aggressive westernization pursued by Dalhousie elsewhere in the subcontinent.

Dalhousie virtually invented a policy termed the "Doctrine of Lapse." He considered all princely states less efficient, more corrupt, less democratic, and less susceptible to reform than the area under his rule; and he was, therefore, determined to consolidate all under his sway. Dalhousie argued that Britain as the paramount power had the right to recognize succession and, if an heir were lacking, to annex the state. Dalhousie insisted that if a natural son were not available, only the Company had the right to decide if an adopted son could succeed the father. If recognition were withheld, then the princely line had "lapsed" and the state passed to the Company as the paramount power. He forcibly applied this doctrine to a number of princely states, arousing a wave of protest and apprehension. Dalhousie was accused of attempting to destroy Hindu states when he also annexed other principalities whose rulers he accused of misgovernment. Together the various annexations looked like an attempt to destroy the remnants of traditional India. Still Dalhousie made the Company and himself the unquestioned arbiter of all within his purview. He even attempted to abolish the old Mughal line by decree, though he was ultimately prohibited from doing so by London.

Dalhousie's legacy was not entirely negative. He built the Grand

Trunk highway from Calcutta to Peshawar as well as many other less ambitious road networks. He introduced telegraphic communications, organized an efficient postal department, and instituted large scale irrigation projects. But the railway system represents the project for which he has been justly remembered. For years railway construction was delayed because London felt railroads might not be profitable. Dalhousie did not succeed in convincing London until 1853, and when he left in 1856, only 200 miles of railway had been completed. Still transport by rail had begun and developed unabated in the years ahead. Railway construction was, however, not entirely a blessing. Railways helped destroy handicraft industry in the interior, for they placed inland markets within easy reach of the machine-made products of the West. Also railways and the crews that built them became agents for the spread of disease that took heavy tolls in villages where resistance to world diseases was low due to isolation from illness associated with most of the globe. The development of railways, coupled with Dalhousie's push for Western education, for roads and telegraphs, and for consolidation, helped spawn what the British called the Mutiny of 1857 or what many Indians term the First War of Indian Independence. By the time Dalhousie left India, in 1856, there was little doubt left in the minds of the inhabitants — India was ruled by Europeans for European interests.

The administrative edifice was European and would continue to become more European for a decade or two. The Company by 1856 was no longer simply one of many states in India; it was virtually the only one. All others were mere shadows of their former selves. Dalhousie made clear to all that native princes were living anachronisms whose life spans were near an end. As Governor-General he had added 150,000 square miles of territory to the Company through consolidation or liquidation of native states.

• 1857 and Its Aftermath

When Dalhousie left India in February 1856, he left behind an empire that seemed quiescent. Yet within a year much of India was ablaze and the empire itself apparently teetered on the brink of dissolution. Why the sudden reversal? Perhaps no one will ever explain it to the satisfaction of all, but the Sepoy Mutiny represented only one of many nineteenth-century resistance movements by subject peoples against Western imperialism. The British practice of lubricating cartridges with animal fat inflamed the religious sensibilities of Muslims and Hindus who composed the Sepoy troops. Muslims, who considered the pig unclean, and Hindus, who considered the cow sacred, understandably refused to handle the ammunition. The first such refusal occurred in January 1857, near Calcutta, and was rapidly followed by others. By the end of the spring, troops stationed in northern India rose in mutiny, seizing control of great inland cities like Delhi. The British responded quickly, treating the protesters as the worst type of traitors, while refusing to admit that too great an involvement in the daily life of the inhabitants had started the conflagration.

When electrifying news of the massacre of European officers by the Sepoy troops in the northern hinterland began filtering into Calcutta, the British, in righteous indignation, responded with a vehemence unmatched during their rule. Administrators viewed it as a struggle between East and West, civilization and barbarity, Christian and heathen. British troops stormed the old Mughal cities and forts which the insurgents had occupied in the land of the upper Ganges, capturing Delhi, the rebel capital, in September 1857. Before another year had passed, they had pacified all of India. By mid-1858 British rule had been restored, but at a great cost in lives and money; and the cruel excesses on both sides during the war left an intense feeling of hate and fear in the hearts of all, native or foreign, for a generation and more.

The Hindu Widows' Remarriage Act of 1856 was a good example of how the Company felt it had the right to change customs in accordance with emancipated Indian views against the traditional Hindu majority. This act gave Hindu widows the right to remarry by law, thus ignoring the orthodox religious leaders who opposed the act. Also the manner in which Hindu College was changed into Presidency College at Calcutta in 1854 was another example of the British attitude which argued that European views and practices were dominant over Indian concerns and interests. Dalhousie knew his policies threatened to remove decision-making from the hands of the elders and to give it to the courts and bureaucracy, which were becoming more Anglicist in outlook with each passing day. Why did he persist? Reaction was bound to come. With their way of life threatened, it is no wonder the indigenous responded violently in 1857. The ranks of the rebels were swelled with the rajas who had been treated poorly, with the former landed aristocracy who were being replaced by English-speaking barristers, and with Muslim and Hindu spiritual leaders who feared the actions more than the teachings of the Western Christian — both missionary and bureaucrat. The widespread uprising was the strongest in places like Oudh, a princely state annexed by the Company only months before the mutiny broke out. The old aristocracy was desperate in Oudh and elsewhere; to them the War of 1857 was an exercise grown out of desperation.

Street market in Goa. Embassy of India, Washington, D. C.

To many the mutiny was simply the last attempt by the old regime, the remnants of the Mughals, to reassert themselves. Undeniably the old order fought to reassert itself and to reclaim lost prerogatives and dignity.

But there was another dimension that cannot be ignored; the mutiny was supported by a large segment of the population that had little to gain from a return to the old order. Many Indians were stirred perhaps by nothing more than frustration. The pace of reform had been too rapid for many. For instance, a requirement issued in 1856 which made it obligatory for all military personnel to serve wherever sent struck a raw nerve. For many a Hindu, a trip across the ocean meant pollution, a loss of caste, or social ostracism. The British too often refused to consider the effects of their actions. They found it easier to attribute opposition and even the uprising to mindless traditionalists, particularly Muslims, who because of their "inferior nature" simply could not comprehend the blessings of European rule, than to evolve a system in which all participated in the decision-making process. Paternal despotism was to the British in India as much a statement of lack of faith in the ability of the indigenous to rule as it was a political system designed to bestow wealth and glory on its inheritors, if not its founders.

The uprising of 1857 caused British officialdom to turn to imperialism; administrators were convinced that it was dangerous to attempt reform of social and religious customs. The government therefore became far less innovative and far more conservative for the remainder of the nineteenth century. The attitude that permeated every level of the I.C.S. was one of *noblesse oblige*, and it clearly intensified as the century wore on. Thus, during the zenith of British rule, 1858-1905, the administration became unabashedly exclusive. Indians were advised to be patient, to watch, to learn; and one day in the distant future the indigenous would be brought into the administration. But first they must learn from their mentors who would, of course, judge when Indians were fit to participate more fully in governing themselves. Thus the Crown, which assumed direct rule in 1858, found it necessary to prove to Indians why their rule was beneficial as well as moral, stable, and Christian. The British came to believe their own myth — the myth that they and they alone could provide the unity and the stability necessary for all to prosper. Indians were deemed unfit by temperament and training for the task.

• Rise of the Middle Class

Since the Crown and its agent, the I.C.S., forsook innovation in favor of the status quo, the initiative and driving force behind change fell to a new class that appeared in strength on the Indian scene in the latter part of the nineteenth century. This group arose and existed on the fringes of British society. For want of a better term its members are often called the Indian Middle Classes. They were native agents by virtue of their broker relationship to the English. But they were not middle class in the European sense of the term; they resembled more a professional intelligentsia. Most of the members of this new group were the lower echelon clerks needed by British administrators as functionaries at the lower levels of government. This group had remained loyal to the British in 1857, for they felt that the British in the long run stood for more enlightened government than did the princes, whom they equated with a return to a feudal age.

• The Hindu Renaissance

In the first half of the nineteenth century, when the middle classes were numerically small, there appeared a group of native intelligentsia who pushed reform of Indian customs and mores every bit as hard as Bentinck. One of the most significant of these was Rammohun Roy, a man often termed the "Father of Modern India." Roy was a social reformer who in the 1820s founded the Brahmo Sabha (Society of God), later known as the Brahmo Samaj, in his native Bengal. Roy re-interpreted Hinduism to his followers. He denounced caste restriction, opposed idolatry, favored women's rights, and stressed monotheism. He also rejected Christianity and the claim by missionaries of the superiority of the Christian ethic. He depicted Christianity as superstitious and stressed the Asian rather than the Western origins of the faith of Jesus. He launched what has been called the Hindu Renaissance.

Roy, who died in 1833, was followed by other notable reformers such as Debendranath Tagore and Keshub Chandra Sen. The most important reformer outside of Bengal was probably Dayananda Saravati (1824-1883). Dayananda founded the Arya Samaj (Society of the Aryans), demanded that all ritual from the past millenia be discarded, and called upon Hindus to return to the *Vedas* as their source of religious and social thought. Though himself a Brahmin, he attacked ritual as stifling and as post-Vedic in origin. He argued that there was no sanction in the ancient *Vedas* for untouchability, child marriage, or the subjugation of women. He ceaselessly attacked idolatry as well as Islam and Christianity, which he viewed as foreign imports, and frequently debated theological points with Muslims and Christians in large public assemblies. Dayananda, like Vivekananda, another zealous reformer of the latter half of the century, urged his followers to take technical knowledge from the West but to dismiss Western religion as inferior to that of the indigenous.

The spiritual reformers of the Hindu Renaissance gave a sense of pride to those long on the defensive. They made them believe they could reform India better than their British overlords and helped lay the basis for a feeling of religious identity in which they could take pride. They could study Western culture in order to better defend their own. Still, the commonality of the rising middle classes was derived as much from exposure to the West as it was from the burning demands for reform that emanated from the religious reformers of the Renaissance. In fact, the English language alone was a cohesive bond for the middle classes. The English language permitted them to speak, write, and communicate with one another on a level never possible in pre-British days.

• Role of the Middle Classes

The British, whose numbers were small, always resented the aspiring middle classes that they had created, possibly because they were as dependent upon them as the new classes were upon their political masters. Indians were needed to administer the empire, and as the British took on more and more responsibilities, a greater shortage of European manpower developed. In the 1880s there were fewer than 90,000 Europeans in all of India, and thousands of these were planters, missionaries, and business-men, while well over 55,000 were army personnel. Administrative manpower was largely drawn from the great urban centers like Calcutta and Madras where schools, anxious to educate their pupils in English, abounded. The Hindus flocked to the schools in order to prepare themselves for administrative positions, while Muslims, on whom the uprising of 1857 was blamed, were slow to respond to the education that became readily available even in the *mofussil* (back country).

The Indian Middle Classes were by the 1880s a new elite, and like elites of any time they were interested in expanding their role in the decision-making process. They began to form organizations to agitate legally for greater participation. Caste organizations designed to help educate caste brethren and schools owned and run by the indigenous began to dot the Indian landscape. This new elite was far different from the old. They were seeking positions in government in order to increase their upward mobility and wealth, and for some time many were little in-terested in obtaining the religious sanction or stamp of approval tradition-ally necessary for acceptance. Their position depended more on marketable skills than on acceptance by princes. Though the middle classes eventually found mobility blocked by both prince and bureaucrat, they considered the British as the lesser of the two evils standing in their path. Thus they found themselves alienated from the old elite and not trusted by the British.

• Political and Cultural Response Among the New Elite

The British were aliens in the empire they had created. They could or would not easily adopt or adapt to a relationship similar to that which evolved in Canada after the British Parliament passed the North American Act of 1867. The implementation of this act offered hope to the rising middle classes, for they rightly viewed the act as the germinal legislation around which dominion type of government would grow. Indian reformers looked to a future date when a British Empire based on mutually beneficial cooperation between its Indian and English components would exist. Most of the new elite accepted for a time the fact that they were not yet ready for full participation; they had remained loyal to the British during 1857 for that reason. The good faith exhibited by the rising class was not reciprocated, and by the 1870s some of the new elite were hoping to prod the British government into change. Surendranath Banerjea began demanding that the administration open its ranks more fully to Indians. Banerjea in 1876 formed the Indian Association as a pressure group designed to gain for its members greater access to the coveted positions in the I.C.S. Banerjea and others hoped to convince their British overlords through legal means to accept cooperation with the aspiring educated classes. The British, however, had turned away from innovation. Their attitude was imperialist in the sense that they felt militarily, technologically, politically, and culturally superior to the non-Western world.

• British Policy in the Princely States

After 1857 the Crown actually attempted to make an ally of the old elite. Past mistakes were blamed on the Company and its overly ambitious and hasty policy. In very rapid succession the Crown abolished the Company, renounced the doctrine of lapse, and accepted princely successors based on traditional law and custom, including adoption. Once emasculated, the old elite were looked on as allies — to be used in the name of the Crown to stifle criticism from the middle classes. After Victoria was officially declared Empress of India in 1877, her Governors-General (now called Viceroys) began to accept the princes as the "spokesmen" for India. This infuriated the new elite, who claimed that right, mostly on the basis of education, for themselves. The "educated and thoughtful" classes now came to resent the princes more than the British, and this made it easy for the British to pose as the objective arbiter between two self-seeking and self-interested classes. Thus the British openly favored in the last half of the century the very group it had labored so hard to destroy, and the class the British had created was the class to which it refused political participation. This change in attitude helped create a class of parasitic princely pensioners, who became more interested in their own survival than in the survival of others, and therefore rather directly helped sow the seeds for the destruction of this princely class in recent years.

• Reform Sponsored by the Educated

Though the British were not successful in restoring the princes to their traditional role, they persisted in the 1890s and thereafter to make membership in newly-constituted councils of the viceroy more readily available to princes than to the educated middle classes. Europeans knew before the end of the century that political activism, if it were to develop, would not emanate from the princes. It would surely arise from the ranks of the newly educated. Men like Banerjea and Mahadev G. Ranade began espousing social and political change in the 1870s in forceful terms. Banerjea, on the east coast in Bengal, and Ranade, in Maharashtra on the west coast, demanded reform of bureaucratic abuses. Both organized societies to "educate" their own and the British to the need for full participation in the future. Their societies and those of others less well-known had as their focus two distinct goals: to educate Indians in the Western style, hopefully in Europe, without being opposed by traditionalists who would stigmatize such persons upon return, and to convince the British to continue to expand openings in the administration for qualified Indians, at the expense of Europeans if need be.

No small amount of time was devoted to reform of traditional structures in Indian society in the period 1885-1914. The educated elite were convinced that social reform had to precede political reform. They felt their requests for greater participation would fall on deaf ears unless they purged themselves of what they considered the disabilities of the past. Many of the educated risked ostracism by marrying outside their caste, by dining with members of other castes, by marrying widows, and by journeying across the ocean to Britain for training. The strictures of the past were most pronounced in the mofussil (back country) where orthodox members of the communities declared outcaste all those who broke the traditional rules, and even men like Motilal Nehru and Mohandas K. Gandhi were at one time considered outcaste by their respective communities. But by the time World War I broke out, the reformers had won the day. The orthodox fell before the onslaught of modernity, but the battle for reform left many scars.

• The Beginnings of Political Activism

In the 1880s B.G. Tilak, the noted traditionalist agitator, was one of many who came to resent the haughty, pretentious, racist attitude of the post-Mutiny administrators. Another was Dadabhai Naoroji, a Parsi businessman, termed the Grand Old Man of the National Movement. Naoroji (1824-1917) provided the rationale for why the British should accept Indians as full participants in the administration of their land. His famous "economic drain theory" held very simply that Britain had grown wealthy and prosperous due to the wealth it drained from South Asia, and that Britain had a moral obligation to help those who had paid and were continuing to pay for her prosperity. The proof of the theory, it was argued, was undeniable. Clive had won the Battle of Plassey in 1757, and the first phase of the Industrial Revolution in Britain commenced in 1760. Indian wealth in incalculable amounts had been "drained" from India to finance British industrialization, it was argued, particularly by youthful Indian barristers who fell under the spell of the Grand Old Man. The younger educated knew the work of the historian, Arnold Toynbee; many had heard him lecture on the origins of the Industrial Revolution, and they had no trouble coupling the teaching of Toynbee with Naoroji. The economic drain theory became a solid basis for the philosophical underpinning of the nationalist movement launched by the new elites. It took little imagination to justify demands for participation in the decision-making process once one felt the process was being subverted by requiring Indians to support a system that existed to serve the interests of Liverpool and Manchester industrialists rather than the native peoples.

• The Founding of the Indian National Congress

Among the many organizations founded by the educated classes to vocalize their claims in the closing decades of the last century, the Indian National Congress stands out as their singular achievement. The Congress, organized in 1885, quickly emerged as the major spokesman of the hopes of the educated classes. It became the vehicle for the independence movement, and no discussion of modern India is complete without some analysis of the importance of its founding and its composition. At the time of its founding, India was seething with discontent prompted by an outcry of protests from the European community in India. Europeans were aroused over a piece of legislation known as the Ilbert Bill. The bill would have permitted Indian judges to preside in cases where Europeans were to be tried; and its introduction, in 1883, during the last months of the administration of Lord Ripon (1880-1884), was the last straw for the European community in India. Ripon had repealed a number of laws hated by Indians, including the Vernacular Press Act, which made it nearly impossible to publish a critical newspaper, and the Arms Act, which required non-Europeans to have a license for arms. The Europeans organized such an outcry over being tried before Indian judges that the bill was withdrawn. The educated Indians, perceiving the advantage in organized opposition, formed the Congress in December, 1885.

For the first ten or fifteen years, the Congress was little more than a part-time debating society. It met only in December, during the Christmas holidays, when government offices were closed, and passed a seemingly endless round of resolutions designed to prod the government towards acceptance of more participation on the part of Indians in the higher echelons of administration. Also for most of its early career, the Congress was little more than a rich man's club. Membership fees were high (about the price of a good tailored suit), and there appears to have been little attempt to bring into the membership people who were non-professional or uneducated. Membership was limited almost solely to the Western-educated, and they labored hard to present a united front on all the major issues of the day in regard to British policy. But close below the surface of the unity and amity theme the Congress so publicly projected lay deep cleavages that were both cultural and political.

• Nationalists vs. the Reformers

A split in the Congress became obvious in the 1890s with the emergence of Tilak as a national leader. Tilak was the first to bridge the gap between "arm chair" politicians and the masses. Tilak was not a liberal; he viewed the British in his nation as aliens who had no right to interfere in socio-religious customs and traditions of the people. Tilak was not willing to see his customs purged or modernized in order to make them more acceptable to those who wielded political power. He wanted a grass-roots alternative to British policy, not a willing acquiescence. Tilak's weapons were tradition and emotion. Armed with these, he started newspapers in Marathi, his language, and launched one editorial crusade after another designed to arouse among his readers a desire to protect their way of life against the onslaught of the British and his opponents, the reformers. His aggressive attacks on the British helped split Congress into two factions, the Moderates (reformers) and the Extremists (nationalists). Just as the Moderates (who had founded the Congress) used meetings as a forum for educating via long Victorian speeches on the virtue of reform,

Tilak came to use Hindu festivals for presenting speeches and dramas which eulogized the Hindu accomplishments of the past. Tilak supported associations designed to prohibit the killing of cows, opposed inoculations against smallpox, and argued that the British had no right to impose an age restriction for marriage.

Tilak's opposition to the British on some issues seemed real. He sincerely believed the British had no right to increase the minimum age for female marriage to twelve from the traditional ten. He did not feel that the age could not be raised; rather he objected to its being raised by the alien British. Though losing the battle over the age limit, in 1891 he won the war. He quickly became one of India's best known heroes, rapidly expanding his base by organizing festivals commemorating Maratha deities and heroes. Every year celebrations with week-long festivals were held in honor of Ganesh, the Elephant God, or Shivaji, the Maratha warrior who had helped destroy the mighty Mughal Empire. Understandably, Muslims were incensed by Tilak, and rioting became a way of life at these festivals. Tilak was not impressed by Muslim protests, however, for the Muslim was almost as great an object of his hostility as the Christian Englishman.

Hindu opposition to Tilak came primarily from G. K. Gokhale, an accomplished debater and leader of the Indian National Congress from the 1890s until his death in 1915. Gokhale and his Moderates were horrified by the violent tone of Tilak's rhetoric. They viewed him as something reborn from the distant past – a symbol of the possible return to the dark days of the medieval world. Tilak, they felt, would not take India forward, for he opposed social reform. Many of the Moderates were Social Darwinists. They felt Indians must prepare themselves first through education, purge themselves of deficiencies in social and political organizations, and only then demand full participation or independence. The Moderates wanted change and participation, but they fully expected it to come slowly. Social and educational preparation had to precede political emancipation. Otherwise, they rationalized, India would become free only to be conquered by another foe, foreign or indigenous. The Moderates believed the British were not their only enemies. The Princes and the Extremists were in many respects much greater foes, for they could undo the work of several generations. The road to modernity was, to the Moderates, a British road. They had to travel it or perish. Tilak would destroy all; he was a communalist (a person interested only in his community's well being). Moderates felt that Tilak as the major spokesman of Hindu Communalism would tear the nation asunder. They viewed the future in terms of separation of church and state; in fact, they argued that a secular state was the only possible way to keep India

Thousands of pilgrims fill the shore at the confluence of the Ganges, Jamuna, and Saraswati rivers during the Hindu festival of Ardh Kumbh. Religious News Service photo.

together — with or without the British. Legal separation of church and state was to the Moderates one of the really positive features of British rule. They wanted to continue it, to extend it; they wished never to risk a confrontation between the Hindu and Muslim peoples.

• The Muslim Response

Muslims were slow to respond positively to the British Raj. At first they were bitter; they were the rulers who had lost an empire. They still held positions in the nineteenth century equal to their percentage of the population, but they had lost the prestige of old. Also the Muslims, for some reason, seemed to withdraw from the world the British were building, at least for the first half of the century. Historical antagonism between Muslim and Christian (which one today often forgets had existed) may account for some of the withdrawal, but not all of it. By mid-century it became clear to many Muslims that the new Hindu elite were entering the new British world willingly. Muslims knew that many of the Hindus actually favored a British over a Muslim government, and a fear of being overwhelmed by Christian/Hindu administrators began to dawn in the consciousness of the Islamic community. Something needed to be done to protect the economic interests of the community. This was not easy in the 1860s and 1870s, for the British believed the 1857 uprising to be primarily the work of Muslims and followed a discriminatory policy in accord with that belief.

It was not until the 1880s that official policy began to change. Part of the explanation for the change may be due to the publications of W. W. Hunter, a bureaucrat turned historian, who argued that Muslims would become a desperate community if the government did not change its attitude toward them. But it must be remembered that changes in the treatment of Muslims by British overlords seem to coincide almost perfectly with the intensification by Hindu middle classes of their pressure for change through the founding of organizations like the Indian National Congress. The change in attitude might also have been due in large measure to the Aligarh Movement, which was spearheaded by Sayyid Ahmad Khan (1817-1898), a man who helped solve for Muslims the problem of how to obtain a Western education without attending the European missionary schools.

Sayyid Ahmad Khan was in the service of the Company during the upheaval of 1857. He remained loyal and became a trusted servant of the Raj. In 1875 he founded Aligarh College in order to provide Muslim youth with a Western education transmitted in an Islamic milieu. His movement helped revitalize his community, and his advice became synonymous with action. Sayyid convinced his Islamic brothers that British rule would not soon pass away and that they must therefore cooperate. He also advised Muslim youth to remain aloof from politics, to study the West, to keep the faith, and to remain outside the Indian National Congress. He argued against helping to democratize the government, for a representative republic would be a government in which the Hindu would dominate. He openly advocated the retention of British paternalism as preferable to a democracy dominated by the majority. Khan advised all Muslims to prove their loyalty to Britain, to be above suspicion, to be apolitical, and to avoid any and all types of agitation. He saw the Muslims as a dominant force only if they tied their destiny to that of the European minority, and he thought one could borrow Western technology while rejecting Western ethics. More importantly, he convinced other Muslim leaders of the wisdom of his way, and the new elite of the Islamic minority entered the twentieth century virtually determined as a group to remain consciously apolitical but bureaucratically influential.

• Problems of Identity

The cultural response of the nineteenth century helped lay the basis for the clear split of the twentieth. The British, who have often been charged with a policy of divide and conquer, used the identity crisis to their own advantage. The British did not create the regional, communal, and linguistic divisions; but they encouraged their widening, in part because neither the Hindu nor the Muslim seems to have understood the identification problem of the other. But communalism was only one of many manifestations at the root of the identity crisis, for in most respects the cultural response under the Raj had been political as well as religious, social as well as economic, and regional as well as national. Tilak had a Hindu as well as a regional appeal. Shivaji was more a regional symbol than a national one. Still Tilak had a national appeal in that he stressed direct action to rid all of South Asia of British influence, though his means alienated the Moderate nationalists, who were devoted to constitutional means.

Thus British India suffered as few states have from diversity of almost every type — linguistic, ethnic, religious, political, social. It was difficult for many to decide what was the first claim on their loyalty. Was a man a Hindu or was he a Bengali, an Indian, a prince, a westernizer, a reformer, an urban dweller, a believer in caste, or was he simply confused? What was to tie his identity together? Was it to be traditional history? Tilak had tried that, but his symbols were all Hindu. How did one overcome it without rejecting one's own culture? Also how could one combat the British assertion that they alone could provide India with peace, unity, and good government? How could a foreign foe provide this, if in fact the Europeans were foes or evil and not worthy of emulation? Also how could one overcome the regional animosity that existed in areas in regard to the Bengali or Madrasi administrators who had pushed into the hinterland and into good positions with British expansion at the expense of the natives of the various regions? Long before the end of the century, citizens of the Punjab and Bihar were launching movements designed to rid their provinces not of Europeans but of people of Bengali lineage.

The administrative unity of Britain seems to have provided little except a channel for feelings in regard to British overlordship. This was, however, a negative feeling. What remained to be done by 1900 was to find a way to direct the negative feeling of being non-European into a positive feeling of being Indian. The positive British contribution to India was one of language, literature, a theoretical love of freedom, and an Anglicized class of elite who had not yet discovered who they were or what they wanted, though they seemed confident that one day they would lead and others would follow. The negative donation of the British was one of hatred. British policy never really attempted to help foster cooperation in the subcontinent. In fact, the British fostered division because it suited their needs. The British won India through cunning and the sword, and they held it by playing off one group against the other. Cooperation was never a conscious British aim after 1857, perhaps never after 1837, and the British must accept no small share of the blame for many of the problems associated today with contemporary South Asia.

3

The Making of Independent India

AS THE NINETEENTH century drew to a close, indigenous India clearly seemed headed for a confrontation with its alien masters. Many Hindu and Muslim leaders of the 1890s were clearly aware that such a clash was inevitable, though they differed widely as to the best policy to be pursued. Some national leaders favored violence, but the overwhelming majority were more inclined to support pressure tactics and agitation of a "constitutional" or legal nature. The latter felt education must precede freedom, and with this in mind wealthy Indians began founding newspapers and colleges. However, the confrontation came long before anyone expected it would, in part because of the nature of the administration of the last of the true imperialist viceroys, Lord George Nathaniel Curzon, a Conservative party leader, who assumed that post in 1899.

• The Curzon Years

The administration of Lord Curzon, from 1899 to 1905, marked both the zenith and the decline of the Raj. He was arrogant, aristocratic, and contemptuous of the Indian National Congress, the middle classes, and all they symbolized. His administration was a climax to the era inaugurated by Dalhousie. Curzon believed in paternal despotism, and his despotism and his high-handed treatment of Indian subordinates became legend. He was responsible for the first mass demonstrations organized in opposition to viceregal policy, and he helped create the environment in which the first rumblings of Indian nationalism were heard.

Percival Spear, the British historian, has argued that Curzon was guilty of a common mistake among post-mutiny administrators. Spear has contended that "the average administrator erred, because he was still looking for Western reform in aristocratic places, and did not perceive the significance of the new rising middle class." Curzon, who "shared in this fallacy," foolishly "provoked by his action a rude awakening." Of course, one can argue with this assessment by pointing out that Curzon was not an average administrator, that he should have recognized the importance of the new elite, and that the rising middle classes were headed for a confrontation with or without Curzon. Still Curzon was the catalyst, for he was so easy to dislike. All nationalists could agree on one feeling — their intense hatred of the Viceroy. Curzon represented all things they disliked in British rule. He was to them a repudiation of progress. Many Britons agreed, and Curzon often found himself at odds with London politicians. Curzon insisted he had to be free of interference, either British or Indian. When London in succession vetoed Curzon's expansionist policy in Tibet and then sided with General Kitchener in a dispute over who should command the army, Curzon indignantly resigned.

Curzon was not long in revealing his sentiments toward the educated middle classes. In his first year in office, he changed the composition of the Municipal Boards that administered the urban centers, a system that dated from the Ripon era. Ripon, who wanted to introduce some measure of self-government, had inaugurated the boards as a training ground for Indians. Two-thirds of the board members were elected indirectly by organizations like Chambers of Commerce, but fully one-third of the members were appointed by the viceroy. Curzon claimed the boards were corrupt and that he could increase their efficiency as well as reform them by reducing elected representation to 50 percent. The middle classes realized the enormous advantage this would give the government, for opposition and a forum for it would be seriously curtailed. Curzon's policy was viewed as an attempt to deny the new elite a role in the governance of their land — and more importantly, an attempt to return the Indian administrative structure to undisguised despotism.

Curzon had a free hand for the whole of his first administration. The educated suffered what they considered to be affront heaped on affront. In 1903-04 Curzon threatened the Bengali educated by introducing the Universities Act, which like his other "reforms" was designed to enhance efficiency at the expense of the autonomy enjoyed by the University of Calcutta. Curzon argued, not unjustly, that Calcutta with its myriads of affiliated colleges was in need of corporate restructuring. His proposal was to improve the administration as well as the nature of the instruction by increasing again the number of appointed members on the governing bodies while reducing the members elected by the faculties. Educated Bengalis knew their positions and wealth were a result of the training received at Calcutta University. They wanted to see the program expanded to produce more educated, not retrenched in favor of graduate education. So when the quality of the persons brought in to replace the educated Bengalis was no better than those replaced, educated Bengalis rose in protest. They found support across India, for others felt such a policy could be used in other schools in India to thwart the aspirations of all. The Universities Act of 1904 opened completely the chasm between the educated and the administrators, and it was never again to close.

- ## The 1905 Partition of Bengal

After completing one five-year term, Curzon was reappointed to a second. Following a summer's rest in Europe, he returned to India in 1904 determined to destroy the Congress and the elite who had dared challenge him. Curzon had written in 1900 that "Congress is tottering to its fall, and one of my great ambitions while in India is to assist it to a peaceful demise." Shortly after returning, with revenge in mind, he announced that the province of Bengal was too large an administrative unit and would be split or "partitioned" into two parts. The immediate reaction to this announcement of administrative restructuring was the organization of "monster petitions" and "monster meetings" to demonstrate displeasure. It was not an unusual reaction, but it was unexpected. Curzon was, however, not to be defeated by "native rabble." He effected partition in 1905; but he won the battle and lost the war. The Curzon partition hastened his end and probably the end of the Raj as well. Bengal was ablaze with political activity such as it had not witnessed in its entire existence. Even the conservative Surendranath Banerjea, now an old man, came forward to lead the Swadeshi Movement.

Swadeshi meant purchase only of those goods produced in India by Indians. Its leaders asked all Indians to boycott foreign goods and picket foreign shops. The European business community became alarmed, and Congress leaders used the agitation to demonstrate for the first time an active and virulent opposition to Curzon. Bengali leaders depicted their "nation" as split — bleeding — into two parts, for the partition created two provinces out of the previous one. The poetry of revolt appeared in which the authors called on Congress to agitate from the Himalayas to Cape Comorin to help rescind the measure. Many in Bengal thought the old province was too large, but they did not want to see the Bengali people living in two provinces. One ethnic group should have, they argued, one province. If partition was necessary, draw the boundary so as to keep most Bengalis in one province. Curzon, however, remained adamant; he would not be pressured by tactics of the street. But the waves of antagonism did not subside as the Viceroy felt they would, and finally in 1912 the Raj rescinded Curzon's action in favor of a new partition which was based on ethnic divisions rather than administrative efficiency.

Unquestionably British officials underestimated the impact the Swadeshi Movement was to have. They were surprised when the movement turned violent. The defeat of Russia by Japan in 1905 had added fuel to activist fires. The Japanese had proved Asians were not inferior to Europeans, and violence came to appeal to a wider spectrum. Revolutionaries like Aurobindo Ghose appeared, demanding that the educated youth give themselves to the task at hand — to free India so that her people could regain their place among the great civilizations of the globe. Sri Aurobindo challenged his fellow nationals to prepare themselves for India's rising, to train themselves for service to a new India, and to master violence if need be so that India might live again as a society free of European domination. Secret organizations began to multiply, even in the back country, where political activity such as that led by Aurobindo had been unknown previously. A new day had dawned.

• The Congress Split

Curzon resigned in 1905, partly as a result of the outcry generated by the Swadeshi Movement, but this was unimportant to many activists. What was important was the failure of the demonstrators to force Curzon to rescind immediately the partition of Bengal. Congress Extremists held the Moderates responsible for the failure, for they depicted the Moderates' caution as cowardice. The Extremists, led by Tilak, demanded activism on the violent anarchist model then prevalent in the West. They accused the Moderates of actually helping prop up the system that had drained India of its wealth and dignity. The proof, they argued, was in action, not rhetoric. The Moderates controlled Congress, but they refused to support even a resolution requesting self-rule, though the Extremists pushed for it regularly at every sitting of that august body.

The Moderates argued that violence was stupid. The best political tactic was constitutional agitation. They thought that breaking the law, even for good reasons, would lead to a chaos similar to that which initially enabled the British to gain control of India. Also the Moderates pointed out that Lord Minto, the new Viceroy (1905-1910), had the support of John Morley, a leading Liberal, who was placed in charge of the India Office in 1906. Both Morley and Minto promised reform and a complete reversal of the Curzon policy. Hoping to reduce the appeal of the Extremists, the Moderates began to support, though not too warmly, the twin ideals of Swadeshi and Swaraj. The term *Swaraj* had several connotations; it could be translated as self rule, independence, dominion status. Gokhale interpreted it to mean participation within the empire, but Tilak's rhetoric gave it an entirely different coloring. Tilak argued that Swaraj was his "birthright" and that he "would have it."

Confrontation between the Moderates and the Extremists was inevitable; it came at the Surat Congress of 1907. At this meeting Tilak's group was forced to adhere to a testament of loyalty and constitutional agitation or face expulsion. The Extremists chose expulsion, and the Moderates remained in control of Congress for the next twelve years. This was made easier than it might have been by the removal of Sri Aurobindo and Tilak from the ranks of open opposition. Aurobindo was accused of complicity in a bombing incident in 1906. He was found innocent in the trial that followed, but shortly thereafter he retired from politics in favor of a life of religious contemplation in Pondicherry, a French enclave, where he lived until his death in 1950. Tilak himself was charged with encouraging sedition in 1908 and sentenced to exile in Mandalay, Burma, where he remained for the next six years. With their leadership in jail or retirement, the Extremists quickly sank into obscurity, while the Moderates successfully regained their prestige.

• Communalism and the Founding of the Muslim League

One of the unexpected results of the Curzon Partition was the founding of the Muslim League. The Congress had been overwhelmingly Hindu from its founding, and part of the protest over Partition centered on the fact that the province of Eastern Bengal had a clear Muslim majority. Muslims resented this protest of Congress and accused it of being thoroughly communalist; their fears were confirmed when communal riots swept across much of Bengal, East and West, in the wake of the 1905 Partition. Many Muslim leaders felt Congress could never serve as their spokesman, though Congress claimed to be the secular spokesman of all. In 1906, a number of leading Muslims gathered to found a league that could vocalize the interests of what they declared to be "a distinct community of our own with additional interests of our own" which, as they clearly argued, were "not shared by other communities."

Moderate Congressmen strongly reacted to the formation of the Muslim League and argued that the Muslims were playing into the hands of the British by making "divide and rule" an easy task. Of course, this is why the Moderates claimed they had opposed the formation of East Bengal in 1905; they argued that Curzon was using the Muslims. Congress wanted only one spokesman for India, Congress, and the founding of other political organizations weakened its role. However, the Viceroy, Lord Minto, did not share the opinions of the Moderates. He became convinced that Muslims needed legal safeguards to protect them from the over-whelming Hindu majority, and he helped write safeguards into the first major reform scheme introduced in 1909.

• The Morley-Minto Reforms

The Morley-Minto Reforms were of momentous importance. They contained a little for everyone but not much for anyone. The Moderate Congressmen were granted a concession they had long desired — a greater role in the policy making. An Imperial Legislative Council was established, and Indians were included in the Executive Council of the Viceroy. Also the Moderates gained their cherished ideal of election as the criterion for membership, and half of the representatives on the Imperial Legislative Council were to be elected. The electorate was not large, for the franchise was limited to interest groups like those of the planters and the chambers of commerce. The reforms relied on a complicated system of indirect elections in order to present a facade of representative government. The Moderates would probably have been highly pleased by the new scheme if provisions had not been made for the introduction of separate and weighted electorates for Muslims. It was these innovations that nearly made the Moderates reject the reforms and that helped drive the wedge of separation between Muslims and Hindus even deeper. Weighted and separate electorates actually came to be a major cause of conflict during the rest of the life of British India.

Weighted and separate electorates meant seats were set aside in the Imperial and Provincial Councils to be held only by Muslims. Also the number of such seats was weighted in order to give Muslims numerical representation greater than their percentage of the population. It should be pointed out that these practices were similar to those used in Britain, where seats in the Commons were set aside for the academic community, the church, Scots, the Irish, and others. British voting patterns as well as representation were tied to their practice of insuring interest-group representation in the councils of government. Most people in Britain had

Mohandas K. (Mahatma) Gandhi (1869-1948). Embassy of India, Washington, D. C.

one vote in 1910, but many could vote also as businessmen, landowners, churchmen, university graduates, and so forth. Britons felt they were applying their time-proven techniques to guarantee that Muslim opinion would be heard in the councils, thus avoiding the possibility of tyranny of the majority.

The Moderates of the Indian National Congress were not willing to accept the contention that circumstances in India and Britain were similar. They protested vehemently, arguing that the Raj was once again attempting to divide and rule. Congress accused the Raj of attempting to institutionalize an ancient tactic. Moderates argued that this was not the reform they had been led to expect in 1907 when they helped quiet the Extremists, and they flirted with the idea of not participating in the elections planned for 1910. Gokhale, however, finally convinced the others that democratic government proceeded to grow from precedent to precedent and that they should get into the Councils and labor for more extensive change. Thus the Moderates accepted the reforms, though they continued to be rankled by the provision that all Muslims (who could meet the property qualification) could vote for Muslim representatives, though the Hindus enjoyed no such provision. Also the fact that Muslims could stand for election to seats on the council not designated as special disturbed Hindus. This meant Muslims could actually win seats, as they did, far in excess of their proportion of the population. If Muslims won seats set aside for general constituencies, they could be assured of increasing their representation.

Thinking that some reform was better than no reform, the Moderates labored to make the reforms work. The first councils sat for three years. In this time Gokhale and the Congress pushed hard their old Muslim-Hindu unity and amity theme while the British began to withdraw from the support they had so recently given to the Indian Muslims, in part because of trouble brewing in the Balkans and the Middle East, where European Christians and Turkish Muslims were waging the Balkan Wars of 1912-1913. Dwindling British support made many Muslims more willing to join actively with their Hindu counterparts in an effort to make the reforms work. Also, both Muslims and Hindus decided separate electorates might be meaningless, so long as Muslims and Hindus worked together to improve their nation. Still the idea that religion could serve as the basis for designating representation was never popular, especially with the Hindu-dominated Congress, and separate electorates remained a burning issue.

• World War I

World War I was an important turning point in South Asian politics. The Moderates, in hope of gaining new reforms, fully supported the British, and Congress leaders stumped South Asia helping to sell war bonds and encouraging men to enlist in service of the Empire. Indian industry supported the war effort wholeheartedly and willingly supplied much of the material needed to pursue the war successfully, while hundreds of thousands voluntarily served on the war fronts. Indians fully expected their aid would be rewarded once Germany was defeated. There were vague promises as to a new round of reforms once the Germans were defeated, and the Moderates were thus little inclined to press for much during the war. They put their faith in British goodwill. Even Tilak, who was released from Mandalay in 1914, followed a fairly conciliatory policy. The six years in prison seemed to have taken its toll on his health, though he quickly re-emerged as a leading politician. His old opponent, Gokhale, died in 1915; but the void he left was filled in part by Annie Besant, an English woman who had first come to India thirty years earlier as a missionary for Theosophy, a religion that quickly won adherents among the educated. During the war Besant and Tilak organized the Home Rule League with the active support of Moderates.

The spirit of cooperation that manifested itself in the early years of the war spilled over into Hindu-Muslim relations. The entrance of the Muslim Turks on the side of Germany was probably a factor in the improved relations between the two communities. Many of India's Muslims had feared British policy in regard to Turkey before the war; now they feared for their religious brothers and the Khalif (Caliph) even more. In the closing days of 1916, the Congress and the League held their yearly meetings jointly in Lucknow. At the Lucknow Conference the two organizations worked out an accord that came to be known as the Lucknow Pact. By its terms, the League accepted the principle of representative government while Congress gave up its opposition to separate electorates in return for a Muslim promise not to contest any seats designated as part of the general electorate. Both organizations also pledged to work together for self-rule.

The Lucknow Conference occurred at a time when all seemed devoted to participation and cooperation between the contending factions. But as the tide of the war began to turn in favor of the Allies, the British seemed to pull back from the vague promises of earlier years. It was not until late in August, 1917, that the British announced they would soon introduce a new reform scheme that would help India move closer to "responsible government." The announcement pleased Indians, for they interpreted it as something they justly deserved. The problem was that when the new Montagu-Chelmsford Reforms were finally presented in 1919, they fell far short of what had been expected for years, and the dismay and disappointment were quickly made known.

• Dyarchy and Gandhi

The Montagu-Chelmsford Reforms of 1919 helped crush the Moderates as a force in Indian life. Long before the reform scheme became law in December, Indians of all political persuasions expressed a fear of

British intentions. S. Sinha, a leading Moderate from Bihar, in a speech before the Provincial Legislature remarked that he was "sick" of the "very essence of the bureaucratic government" which in its "own infallibility" argued that it did "for the people not what they want, but what they ought to or are supposed to want." The reform scheme was too little, too late. In 1905 Indians would probably have heralded its implementation as a giant step forward. But 1919 was not 1905, and many felt Sinha was correct when he argued that the quality of Indian life would improve only if its Indian citizens "agitate, agitate, agitate; inform, inform the Indian people . . . and inform the British people of the rights of the Indian people and why they should grant them."

The problem was not what Indians wanted in 1919; the argument was over how best to obtain it. Constitutionalists like Sinha wanted "to agitate and agitate on constitutional lines till our people . . . become permeated with one uniform idea." Others claimed the time for education was at an end; it was time for action. The British, most Indian politicians felt, would never willingly hand over the reins of government, even though the reforms promised to consider such a proposal in the future — after the British decided how well the reforms had worked. The reforms were liberal in the sense that they provided for the organization of various councils and assemblies at the national and provincial level in which two-thirds or better of the members would be elected through a widely-increased franchise. A principle, dubbed "dyarchy," was written into the reforms, but it was viewed with skepticism. Dyarchy meant Indians could help administer, could help legislate, but could not have authority over crucial subjects or departments like police, revenue, and finance. Ultimate authority in these areas as in foreign affairs rested with the administration. In other words, Indians were to continue as second-class citizens behind a facade of representative government. Also the heavy principle of weighted and separate electorates was preserved, though it was disguised by setting aside additional seats for members of the Christian, Parsi, Sikh, and Anglo-Indian communities. But the most telling reason why the 1919 reforms were unacceptable centered on the hostile atmosphere that existed after March, 1919, when the government passed the famous Rowlatt Acts. The Rowlatt Acts armed officials with the power of preventive detention. Anyone considered dangerous could be imprisoned, without being charged, purely on the basis of suspicion of sedition or disruptive activities.

● The Rowlatt Acts and the Mahatma

The Rowlatt Acts made even the best British proposals suspect.

Probably no other single piece of legislation so antagonized Indians. Mohandas K. Gandhi, a gifted London law graduate and defender of Indian worker rights in South Africa, rightly termed the Rowlatt legislation "unjust, subversive of the principle of liberty, and destructive of the elementary rights of the individual." The Moderates could not have expressed the view any better; they did, however, disagree with Gandhi over the tactics that should be employed to dissuade the British. Gandhi, who had developed the basic tactics of non-violent resistance in South Africa, called for what he termed a "hartal" as a visible demonstration of displeasure at the government's reversion to paternal despotism. The hartal, or enforced suspension of all economic activity, was a tactic that Gandhi had mastered long before 1919, and it was no idle threat. Gandhi had gained world fame in Africa with the application of hartal tactics, and his naming of April 6, 1919, as the day for a total general strike marked his entry into the Indian political arena.

Gandhi had returned to India in 1915 after years of struggle in Africa for the rights of Indians. At the time he was admired and respected by Europeans and Indians. He announced he would remain aloof from politics for a year in order to ease back into the nation, and he was slow to respond to overtures and entreaties asking him to take up the struggle for Indian rights in India. But Gandhi was drawn into politics quickly as a result of the Lucknow Conference in 1916. At Lucknow, a Bihari peasant asked Gandhi to come to the Champaran District of Bihar to help alleviate the suffering of the peasants who, much against their will, were being terrorized into submission by a landlord class of planters, mostly European. When Gandhi appeared in Champaran, officials attempted to intimidate him with the threat of imprisonment; but he refused to leave the province, announcing that he was perfectly willing to be imprisoned for what he considered right. The provincial administration did not know how to handle the man now openly called the *Mahatma* (great soul), so they forced the planters to accept new laws and rules which favored the peasants. The planters viewed the actions of the government as cowardice and said so often and vehemently. Gandhi's success in Champaran made him feared by the bureaucrats, hated by the planters, and loved by the peasants. Gandhi had long commanded respect; now respect turned to adoration in the hearts of many. Gandhi became *the* Mahatma, and the masses traveled far and wide for a *darshan* (glimpse) of him. In the tradition of old he began to hold *darbars* (audiences) in order to hear the grievances of the oppressed.

The Gandhi decision in 1919 to oppose the Rowlatt Acts by breaking unjust laws frightened many, both Indians and Europeans. They had admired his work in Africa; they feared its consequences in India. The Moderates wanted to wage war against the Rowlatt Acts in the councils and courts. Gandhi wanted to confront the government on his terms, not on theirs. Gandhi was an activist, though he always claimed Gokhale was his *guru* (mentor or teacher). He was not a Tilak, however, for he did not believe the end justified the means. In fact, Gandhi did not wish to win a victory if the means used were questionable. Gandhi was an immensely moral activist who nonetheless removed politics from the parlors of the elite and presented it to the masses in the streets and villages of India, where it had far greater results than any elite movement previously had dared dream.

Gandhi's hartal left violent clashes in its wake. Tension grew especially intense in Amritsar, the capital of the Punjab, where meetings and demonstrations were held though expressly forbidden by the provincial government, which placed the province under martial law. General Reginald Dyer was called upon to restore "law and order" after riots broke out in protest to the "preventive detention" and deportations of two politicians. On April 13, 1919, Dyer learned of a meeting being held in Jallianwallah Bagh, a garden enclosed on three sides by small walls and houses. The General hurried to the one entrance to the Amritsar garden and filled it with his most trusted soldiers. Without any advance warning, he ordered his fifty armed men to open fire on those congregated. They, as obedient soldiers, fired until the ammunition was entirely consumed. It took about ten minutes. General Dyer then ordered his men to leave. Behind lay nearly four hundred dead and twelve hundred wounded. The soldiers had been remarkably accurate. With only 1650 rounds of ammunition at their disposal, they had managed to wound or kill nearly 1600.

Gandhi was horrified, as were many others. Gandhi had been accustomed to launching hartals in Africa with trained men who knew better than to resort to violence such as invited the imposition of martial law in Amritsar. Gandhi, admitting that he had committed a "Himalayan Blunder," called off all hartal activity, and began to cooperate with the government. Gandhi needed peace to train his followers. Also he wanted to give the government every opportunity to discipline General Dyer. Instead Dyer was knighted, and a committee of inquiry exonerated him. The exoneration was the last straw; Gandhi became convinced that the Raj was not capable of being fair, and his faith in British justice nearly evaporated. Indians who had long respected Gandhi were now drawn to follow him. The Amritsar Massacre had given birth to Indian nationalism. India was now more than a hope or aspiration; it was a reality — four hundred martyrs had made it so.

• Congress and Non-Cooperation

The Amritsar Massacre turned Congress permanently away from cooperation with the British and catapulted Gandhi into the role of the leader of the Nationalist Movement. By mid-1920 Gandhi called for total resistance and was promising "Swaraj within the year" if everyone cooperated. By the end of that year Congress had voted to accept non-cooperation as the policy, and *Satyagraha* (the force of truth) was quickly added to the political vocabulary of India. Satyagraha, the name Gandhi gave to his movement, quickly swept aside the opposition.

Gandhi ignited the fires of resistance as no Indian has before or since, partly because his talents extended far beyond the simple utopian dreamer some of the old politicians saw in him. He was an organizer, and he quickly set about restructuring the Congress into an effective tool of nationalism. He based the new organization on a format not far different from Lenin's democratic centralism. He organized local committees at the lowest levels, which in turn elected state groups which finally chose the All-India Working Committee. A part of that organization formed the small Executive Committee which acted as coordinator when Congress was not in session. Gandhi thus organized a well-integrated Congress on the remains of the old.

His followers were asked to become full-time revolutionaries for the cause of freedom. Lawyers heeded the call to boycott the courts, students left their colleges, and politicians spurned the councils newly organized by the 1919 reforms. Famous men like Rabindranath Tagore, India's literary genius and Nobel Prize winner, renounced their titles, honors, and awards, and returned pensions and decorations to the government which had bestowed them. Total anarchy seemed to threaten. Yet the British Raj weathered the storm, even after many Muslims began to join the man Winston Churchill once dubbed a "naked Fakir."

By 1922 it was clear that Gandhi had seized the initiative from the British. He and the Congress represented India, not the British and their reform schemes. Gandhi had turned the Congress into a party with a mass following by setting the membership fee at four annas (a few pennies) rather than the previously high forty rupees. For a few cents one could claim membership in the organization of the mighty, even if one was not inclined to join in the *satyagraha* campaigns themselves. Gandhi was able to create among the masses a sense of identity with the Congress leaders, enabling that body to rely on popular support rather than on the benevolent attitude of the government. Not to join the government became a source of pride and accomplishment, and an expectation of ultimate success inspired the members of Congress. A euphoric optimism developed that was not shattered till 1922 when Gandhi called off the first great non-cooperation campaign because some village followers in Chauri Chaura killed twenty-two Indian policemen during a tax boycott. In calling off the movement, Gandhi again admitted to having committed a Himalayan Blunder in encouraging peasants who were not fully trained in non-violence to take part in the campaign. But in so doing, Congress and Gandhi also lost political momentum, and in the years ahead this was difficult to regain.

Gandhi's followers, thousands of whom were in prison, could not believe that he had called off the movement just when it appeared that they might be successful. Avid supporters called on him to reverse his decision, but Gandhi remained adamant. The people, he reasoned, were not ready, and he was not about to plunge his nation into uncontrolled violence, lest Chauri Chaura be re-enacted. Gandhi announced the time had come for "constructive programs." Though badly confused, Congress accepted Gandhi's decision and helped launch a program of reform. Congress Committees began to teach people how to weave their own cloth. Homespun cloth, called *khadi,* thus became more than a symbol of revolt. Gandhi, however, seemed to take little interest in the Congress he had created. He announced his retirement from politics and devoted the next few years to improving the lot of the untouchable, whom he had renamed *Harijans* (God's children.)

• The Simon Commission and the Demand for Independence

With Gandhi in retirement, the Congress split over policy. Some Congressmen were alarmed by the fact that members of the newly-formed Liberal Party were beginning to monopolize the bureaucratic positions they had rejected. Some leaders decided to organize a party within Congress; it was named the Swaraj Party. The Swarajists contested elections, while others who kept true to the boycott by remaining aloof from government came to be termed the "no-changers." The quiet that crept over India in the next several years was deceiving. The British came to feel they had persevered; the reforms of 1919 seemed to be working. In 1927-1928 Britain sent the Simon Commission to India to study how well dyarchy was functioning. By the terms of the 1919 reforms a commission was not to make such a study until 1929. But the British were so pleased with themselves that they decided to send it early. It was a mistake from the start, primarily because the committee had no Indian members.

When the Commission arrived in India, it found itself heavily embroiled in a boycott. Congress openly disdained the hearings of the Simon Commission so as to demonstrate its displeasure at the all-European composition of the committee. Congress understandably was angered because a committee that was to help decide the future of India had no Indian members. This was again viewed as an affront to all the indigenous and a reassertion of the age-old racism of the past. The Congress action angered the British, and following the report of the Simon Commission the government announced its intention in 1929 to convene a Round Table Conference in London to decide on how best to introduce Dominion status for India. Congress at its 1929 sitting and under the leadership of Jawaharlal Nehru rejected the plan and instead called for complete and total independence. A resolution empowering the Central Committee to launch a second great campaign of civil disobedience was passed. Before long, the battle lines were drawn once again, and Congress declared January 26, 1930, to be Independence Day. All India also was electrified when it learned the Mahatma had been induced to return to lead the campaign.

• The Dandi Salt March

Gandhi, back from retirement, sought to provoke the government. He knew he needed a symbol around which to rally the masses. He found the answer to his needs in salt. The British Raj not only forbade anyone to produce salt, as it was a government monopoly; it also required all to pay a salt tax. The law fell hard on all, particularly the poor, who could least afford to pay much for a necessity of life. Gandhi proposed a 240-mile march from his *ashram* (commune) to Dandi, a city near the sea, where he proposed to break the law by producing salt from sea water. He commenced with few walkers, but the enormous publicity that surrounded the twenty-four-day march encouraged thousands to join the trek. By the time Gandhi reached the sea he was again the uncontested head of Congress. Before long thousands were again in prison, including Gandhi, where many remained for the better part of the next two years, martyrs to the cause of freedom. This Second Civil Disobedience campaign virtually robbed the British of any goodwill they hoped to gain from the First Round Table Conference. The Viceroy, Lord Irwin, decided Gandhi had to participate in such a conference and ordered his release. Gandhi attended the Second Round Table Conference as the sole Congress representative. The Second Round Table Conference, like the first, ended in dismal failure, mostly because the British refused to accept the claim that Congress represented India rather than the Liberals, princes, and others also invited to attend the conference. Gandhi returned to India and to prison.

• The Politics of Communalism

No man ever stirred India as did Gandhi; *Satyagraha* gave meaning to millions. Students found purpose in life, men rediscovered a lost dignity, and bored women discovered a sense of meaningful participation in street politics and in the constructive works of the movement. The masses were exposed to the mainstream of political life. The elites sensed their mission was drawing to a successful conclusion. Non-cooperation became a way of life to millions, and it significantly revolutionized India politically. British intransigence became the object around which a sense of Indian identity developed and flowered between World War I and World War II. The elites of Gandhi's youth may have sown the seed of nationalism, but they were incapable of the harvest. In the 1930s Gandhi became the living representative of resurgent India, nationally and internationally. His fame resembled a clear lake in which millions could bathe and bask in reflected if not participated glory. Muslims were alienated by the success of Gandhi; they saw little to admire in the Hindu ascetic. His Sanskritized vocabulary was foreign to them, and *ahimsa* (non-violence to living things), the source of his philosophy, they viewed as Hindu or Jain. Muslims could not identify with it.

Thus Gandhi, in finding the key to mass identification, also unleashed Muslim fears. The more Gandhi succeeded, the greater the Muslim apprehension became. No Muslim could accept the Gandhi proclamation that the *Bhagavad Gita* and the Sermon on the Mount were the great pieces of didactic literature. Nor could he identify with the image of poverty Gandhi so consciously cultivated. Terms like Swaraj, Swadeshi, and Satyagraha had a very non-Muslim ring. Gandhi's symbols were primarily Hindu symbols, and they evoked primarily a Hindu response. Gandhi knew this, and he searched for symbols which might tie Muslims to his movement. The treaty settlements of World War I which dismembered the Turkish Empire conceivably might provide a common ground. Muslims feared the British might not treat the Caliph with kindness; victors seldom exhibit such a quality to the vanquished. The dismemberment of the Turkish state looked like the first step in such a policy, and for a time it appeared that Gandhi had found the symbol in the Khilafat (Caliphate) Movement which Congress vigorously supported. The movement, however, fell apart when the Turkish ruler Kemal Attaturk abolished the Caliphate in 1924, after having left the office fall vacant two years earlier.

The failure of the Khilafat Movement resulted in a revitalization of the Muslim League. Many Muslims felt the famous "inner voice" Gandhi followed was a Hindu voice. The future founder of Pakistan, Muhammad Ali Jinnah, expressed it clearly when he said, "Inner voice be damned." By the mid 1920s the Hindu-Muslim split was complete. Some Muslim leaders remained loyal to Congress, Gandhi, and secularism; but most clearly supported the Muslim League. Some like Jinnah, who was an old Moderate and once a leading spokesman of amity and unity, forsook both groups. Jinnah even spurned India and took up residence in Britain where he practiced law for some years. While in Britain, Jinnah came under the spell of Muhammad Iqbal, a poet who had a dream. The dream was to have a separate nation, a land of the pure, where Indian Muslims could live peacefully under an administration of their own. Jinnah was reluctant to join Iqbal at first because he felt, as did most old Moderates, that politics should not be based on religion. That, he had always argued, was one of the failings of Gandhi. When he returned to India, however, Jinnah returned to a region dominated by symbols he detested. Everywhere he looked there were pictures of spinning wheels, people clothed in *khadi* (cottage-made cloth), and politicians wearing the famous Gandhi caps. And in the months it took to re-establish Jinnah's ascendancy over the Muslim League, communalism was everywhere on the rise. Jinnah and his people were never able to accept the Nehru argument that communal antagonisms were simply economic in origin. Before long Jinnah became an outspoken advocate of Pakistan.

• The Government of India Act of 1935

Rising communalism poisoned the climate for change, yet it was in this milieu that Britain introduced the most far-reaching legislation in the history of Congress-Raj relations. The expense of administration, not to mention the world image of Gandhi, led to a willingness to grant the substantial changes included in the 1935 act, which provided for the introduction of responsible or ministerial government in the provinces. The act also envisaged the creation of a federation with the Princely States participating, though this never came about due to a failure of the princes to support it. Also the voting franchise was extended to include the participation of well over 25 percent of Indian adults. Congress was forced to admit this act had substance, though it was critical of the continuation of special electorates and the federation principle, which gave new life to the princes. Congress stood for unitary government along secular lines. Gandhi himself had in 1932 renewed his commitment to this through a

Jawarharlal Nehru, Prime Minister of India (1947-1964). Embassy of India, Washington, D. C.

"fast until death" which caused the British to revoke the special electorates planned for the untouchables.

Though reservations were large, Congress decided to participate in the elections for the newly-organized provincial legislatures. As expected, Congress overwhelmed the opposition, especially the Muslim League. When ministries were organized to run the provinces, Congress stuck to the principle innate in the 1935 Act and argued that the new ministers must be drawn entirely from the party of the majority. Jinnah's request that some Muslims be included in Congress provincial governments when they took office in 1937 was abruptly rejected. Congress was not interested in coalition, especially with the Muslim League. The election, they argued, represented a rejection of the League's divisive communalism; Congress spoke for all — Hindu, Muslim, Parsi, Jain, Sikh, and Christian. The Congress attitude made the break complete; Jinnah was now convinced that a separate nation was the only solution.

• Last Days of the Raj

The Congress Ministries labored for two years to prove they could run the provincial administrations as well as the British. Then, in 1939, World War II broke out, and the Imperial government via the Viceroy's statement declared India at war with Germany without even consulting Indian leaders. Congress viewed this as a deliberate insult, especially since the Viceroy had promised prior consultation on all major decisions when Congress took charge of the provincial administrations. The Indian National Congress decided the time for independence was at hand. It offered to support the war effort fully in return for a promise of complete independence upon the successful conclusion of the war. When the British refused, the Congress Ministries resigned en masse, an act that Britain's Prime Minister Churchill viewed as nearly treasonable. There matters stood until 1941.

The Japanese attack on Pearl Harbor on December 7, 1941, helped bring India into the war and into the last major confrontation with the Raj. Both the United States and China needed India as a base for operations against the Japanese. They felt Congress support was essential, and both nations began pressuring Churchill for a conciliatory move. After Chiang Kai-shek, the Chinese Nationalist leader, visited India in February 1942, Churchill decided to send Sir Stafford Cripps to offer the olive branch. The Cripps Mission was a disaster, for he was empowered only to promise dominion status upon conclusion of the war. Congress leaders realized Britain had her back to the wall; the war in Europe was going poorly. Congress wanted independence now and not on terms offered by Cripps. Congress wanted to inherit a united state; Cripps insisted any province that did not want to be a part of a future Dominion of India must have the right to remain apart from it. Cripps was especially concerned that the Princely States should not be forced into an Indian Republic against the will of their rulers. But the Cripps proposal was viewed as a concession to the ideal of Pakistan, which the League had fully endorsed and made a part of their program in 1940. The Congress, in 1942, absolutely opposed the formation of a Muslim state. When discussions with Cripps failed, Congress launched its last great civil disobedience, the Quit India Movement. The movement had as its slogan "Do or Die," and Gandhi, the practitioner of non-violence, observed that India might actually profit from the death of a million to the cause of freedom. Gandhi, now an old man, had given India nationalism; now he wanted to give it freedom. Instead, he and most of the Congress were imprisoned for the rest of the war. Some militant nationalists like Subbas Chandra Bose left the country and allied themselves with the Japanese in an attempt to liberate India through invasion. But India remained chained to an outdated imperialism while Britain waged a war in Europe in the name of freedom. The incarceration of Congress leaders meant the end of passive resistance as a viable force in India. By the end of World War II violence seemed near. India, it became clear, could only be held by force, and by the war's end, the British were exhausted, mentally and financially. Also the Conservative Party lost the election in Britain in 1945, and the Labour Ministry of Clement Atlee was willing and almost eager to get out of India. In 1946 the British sent a delegation known as the Cabinet Mission to negotiate a transfer of power.

The Cabinet Mission proposed the creation of an Indian union rather than a unitary state. In the union the central government's jurisdiction would correspond to that of the Raj, while the provinces were to be grouped into three regional entities, one of which closely resembled the region Muslims demanded for Pakistan. Congress disliked the proposal but accepted it, as did the League. Nehru, who was President of Congress, realistically announced his support with the observation that it made little difference, because once the British were gone Indians would determine what their destiny should be. The Nehru line stirred Muslim fear afresh, and the Muslim League abrogated its previous acceptance in favor of Partition of the Indian subcontinent. Communal riots and massacres began to flare up; the British insisted independence was at hand. Lord Louis Mountbatten, former commander of the wartime China-Burma-India Theater, was appointed Viceroy in early 1947 to preside over the transition. Congress reluctantly agreed to Partition based on a plebiscite; citizens of British India were to vote for union with Pakistan or union with India. The rulers of Princely States were to decide whether they would join one of the new nations or remain independent. On August 15, 1947, power was formally transferred to native rule, and the long chapter in British Indian history came to a close.

● The Nehru Years

Partition aroused hopes and fears seldom matched in history. Millions of people began to migrate to the new states. Waves of anarchy snuffed out the lives of tens of thousands, including that of Gandhi himself, who was felled by the bullet of a Hindu fanatic on January 30, 1948. The uncontrolled violence long feared had come, and "the old India hands" claimed they knew it all along — South Asians could not rule the subcontinent. Churchill seemed to have been correct when he termed the leaders "men of straw." Between twelve and fifteen million are estimated to have migrated after Partition, with about 60 to 65 percent coming to India and 35 to 40 percent going to Pakistan. For years great migrant camps dotted the landscape of the big urban centers like Delhi. Nehru, who as Prime Minister and President of Congress had acquiesced and accepted Partition in order to prevent violence, was visibly shaken. But he and his most trusted ally, Sardar Patel, were determined to build a strong and free India, despite the passion and destruction of the hour.

Patel was a master at negotiation and pressure tactics; he had proved this often during the Satyagraha campaigns. He now called upon all his skills to help integrate the Princely States into independent India. This was difficult because the agreements made in 1947 specifically allowed for the Princes to remain independent, to join Pakistan, or to join India. Paramountcy lapsed with the end of the Raj, through the legal and mutual consent of all; Mountbatten had declared it could not be transferred. Most of the princes were pressured into signing an "Instrument of Succession," the terms of which joined their territory to that of India. Only a few joined Pakistan. The prominent princes were not easily intimidated, and by the time freedom came they had not yet decided whether or not to "accede." The largest of the Princely States was Hyderabad; there a "spontaneous" rebellion, actually sponsored by Congress, erupted, demanding accession to India. The Indian Army was "forced" to intercede in the name of peace. Some Pakistani leaders protested, but there was little they could do. Hyderabad had an overwhelming Hindu population, and it was located in the middle of India. The fact that its Muslim Nizam (prince) refused to yield to "popular" desire was depicted in India as a simple case of intransigence; but another of the Princely States whose ruler refused to accede posed a much more difficult problem.

The ruler of Kashmir was a Maharaja (Hindu Prince), but his people were overwhelmingly Muslim. Also Kashmir bordered both of the new nations. In the hysteria of late 1947, Pakistani tribes invaded Kashmir. The

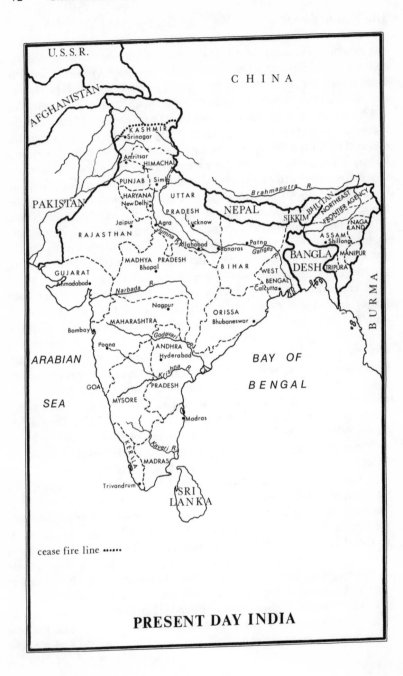

U.S.S.R.

CHINA

AFGHANISTAN

KASHMIR
Srinagar

Amritsar HIMACHAL
PUNJAB Simla
HARYANA
New Delhi

PAKISTAN

UTTAR
PRADESH

Jaipur
Agra
Lucknow

RAJASTHAN

NEPAL

Brahmaputra R.

BHUTAN
SIKKIM NORTHEAST
FRONTIER AGENCY
NAGA
LAND
ASSAM
Shillong

Allahabad
Banaras
Ganges
Patna

BIHAR

WEST
BENGAL
Calcutta

BANGLA
DESH
TRIPURA MANIPUR

MADHYA PRADESH
Bhopal

GUJARAT
Ahmadabad

Narbada R.

Nagpur

MAHARASHTRA

Bombay

ARABIAN

SEA

Poona
Godavari

ANDHRA
Hyderabad

Krishna R.

ORISSA
Bhubaneswar

BAY OF

BENGAL

BURMA

GOA

MYSORE

PRADESH

Madras

KERALA
Kaveri R.

MADRAS

Trivandrum

SRI
LANKA

cease fire line ••••••

PRESENT DAY INDIA

Maharaja decided to accede to India and sent word to Nehru. Indian and then Pakistani troops poured into the area, and a full scale war erupted. Finally, in 1949, a cease-fire line was established with the help of the United Nations. This line, which provided India with the lion's share of Kashmir, has changed little in the intervening years, and war has raged over the region intermittently ever since. The nation which holds Kashmir has a grip on much of Pakistan, which lies to the south, and India has never retreated from the claim that the Maharaja's accession has given it the legal and moral rights of sovereignty. India has refused to consider a plebescite in the area, though it has been often proposed by many, because it argues that Kashmir is an integral part of the nation. After having settled most of the pressing questions with Pakistan to his advantage, Nehru moved to remake India. Among other things he was a Fabian Socialist and quite unlike Gandhi. Gandhi loved, understood, and typified traditional India. Nehru did not. Nehru represented the best of both worlds, but possibly felt comfortable in neither. He had been reared in Britain, schooled in Cambridge, and trained in jail. He was a universalist who felt all men could be brothers, and his philosophy is clearly imbued in the Constitution of India that took effect on January 26, 1950. By its terms universal suffrage came to India, untouchability was legally abolished, and ministerial government on a European model was institutionalized.

Still the years in which Nehru dominated India (1947-1964) were years of economic growth. He introduced economic planning and, through various Five-Year Plans, managed to develop much of the infrastructure necessary for the vitality of an industrial state. Nehru poured funds into dams, railroads, power plants, and irrigation projects. As a result, India is today one of the major industrial states in the world.

Tragically Nehru's successes contributed to India's decline through the 1960s. In his early years Nehru could pose as the leader of the Afro-Asian Bloc and could call for new nations to follow his policy of non-alignment. The Indian poverty of 1947 could, with no small justification, be blamed for some years on the British; but as the years passed Nehru had to share responsibility.

Nehru spent for education, electrification, and hygienic reforms while allocating virtually nothing for military hardware. His international reputation was based on the fame India gained as the workshop of non-violent resistance, not on international realities, and every success seemed to add to the spiraling population. Social and hygienic reforms lowered the death rate dramatically while the birth rate lowered only slightly. The eradication of malaria, one of the major accomplishments of the Nehru years, amounted to a curse. More living bodies meant more poverty. At the time of Nehru's death, in 1964, India was not as well off economically in terms of real per capita income as it had been at the time of his birth. India was free and democratic, the nation had industry, the people lived longer, and illiteracy was in retreat. But India was still a long way from economic self-sufficiency, and freedom from want is today in India a cherished goal of all its people.

• India Today

From January, 1966, through March, 1977, Indira Gandhi, daughter of Jawaharlal Nehru, was Prime Minister. Like her father, she seemed most skilled in foreign policy and again found Pakistan her most difficult problem. However, Indira moved India away from a low military profile and a non-alignment policy. India's detonation of an atomic bomb during her era virtually signaled its arrival as a great power, at least in Asia. Indira successfully played a major international role. In 1971-1972 she intervened in a war between East and West Pakistan which helped free East Pakistan from the latter's domination. Her effort brought on war with West Pakistan; but India won easily, creating the independent nation of Bengla Desh from the conquered Muslim state. But her most significant commitment in foreign affairs came in 1971 when she negotiated a treaty of non-aggression and mutual aid with the Soviet Union. This action made the Bengla Desh intervention possible, gained Russian support for Indian hegemony in South Asia, and secured protection from China, a state deeply distrusted by both India and the Soviet Union.

Domestically, Mrs. Gandhi did not match her success in foreign affairs. She had to contend with opposition in Congress, with linguistic politics that threatened dissolution, and with new movements like those of the Naxalbari. The Naxalbari revolutionaries, dedicated to class warfare, utilized political assassination to spread fear and violence throughout the land. Indira, however, rigorously attacked the most basic of India's problems, the population explosion. Her predecessor Lal Bahudur Shastri, like her father before him, had placed too much faith in economic planning and industrial development at the expense of agriculture and family planning. Mrs. Gandhi reversed these priorities. She hoped to stabilize India's population and improve agricultural production to the point where India would be self-sufficient in foodstuffs.

Indira, however, attempted to deal with India's problems in part by strengthening her political position at the expense of the constitution and especially the legislative branch. With the support of her party she suspended basic civil rights, largely to stifle criticism. Though she

Indira Gandhi, Prime Minister of India (1966-1977).

successfully attacked inflation, she also assaulted her critics by temporarily silencing, intimidating, or even imprisoning them in many cases. Publishers of newspapers and periodicals as well as radio and television broadcasters were systematically censored. Even prominent elder statesmen like J. P. Narayan were forcibly detained for months without trial. Though the direction and substance of her policy remained unclear, there is little doubt that Indira refused any longer to tolerate the free exchange and public criticism suffered by her father for nearly two decades.

Indira felt confident that the nation approved of her forceful actions. Thus, following a two-year period in which her ministry ruled under extra-constitutional powers granted by a series of emergency decrees, Indira in mid-January, 1977, announced that elections would be held two months hence. At the time her position seemed secure. But once she eased press censorship, Indira saw that her standing with the electorate had waned considerably since 1972, when victory over Pakistan had climaxed her popularity. Her ministers failed to perceive that confidence in the regime had eroded steadily. The government had felt emboldened by its efforts to redistribute the land, abolish bonded labor, and reduce rural indebtedness. In fact, Indira's ministry had ameliorated a number of acute problems, inflation being foremost among those addressed most successfully. However, Indira and her government did not survive the ultimate test, the elections of March, 1977.

Had she not silenced her political opponents and stifled the press, Indira might have been informed that confidence in the regime was steadily eroding. For instance, her opponents clearly saw the increasing animosity generated through an aggressive birth control program. Within a few days of the announcement of the forthcoming elections, leading opposition parties met and merged into a political coalition called the Janata Party. Morarji Desai, a former member of the government who had been purged from the Congress Party ranks by Indira a couple of years earlier, led the new coalition. Though Mrs. Gandhi provided only six weeks for the campaign, the Janata effectively closed ranks against her. Politicians who formerly opposed Desai merged under his leadership into one united front. The success of the Janata union stemmed largely from the popular fear that the elections offered the last opportunity to save democracy in India.

The "do or die" determination generated by the Janata soon brought results. Jayaprakash Narayan, a politician with a saintly image and one long critical of Congress corruption, joined Desai and added considerably to the prestige of the organization. Also, Jagjivan Ram, a Congress leader and one of Indira's own ministers, resigned from the government and joined the opposition. During the campaign, Indira's critics also accused her of faulty administration during her tyrannical rule. The Janata concentrated their attacks on Indira's son, Sanjay, and his connection with a government project to produce an inexpensive automobile, a "people's car." When the scheme failed, it collapsed amid charges of corruption and incompetence. Also, Sanjay had been identified with the government program of population control, now immensely unpopular throughout the sub-continent. The Desai coalition's campaign for a restoration of democracy paid large dividends. Sanjay was successfully depicted as the symbol of Indira's reign, as a wayward son, and as a blundering incompetent at best and a worthlessly ambitious sibling at worst. The good harvests of recent years, the decline in prices, the new legislation, and success in foreign affairs did not provide her with the favorable image she had expected. The critics, rather than Indira, won a mandate from the electorate.

Most of the voters believed the Janata; they feared Indira would institutionalize an authoritarian regime. Mrs. Gandhi herself helped create this impression, for she made martyrs of many of her opponents. Rural India, in particular, viewed Narayan as the embodiment of the saintly tradition of Gandhi. His arrest and imprisonment had been deeply resented, and his martyr's image protected from attack all who basked in his reflected glory. When the tabulations were completed, Janata and its allies had 328 of the 542 seats in the Lok Sabha (the lower house). Congress, the party of Indira, could claim only 153 places. Mrs. Gandhi herself lost her seat. The Congress Party supremacy, enjoyed for thirty years, had ended.

Following their victory, the coalition quickly organized a government including more disparate elements than heretofore. It is still too early to assess how well the new ministry will perform. Certainly the Janata has managed to bring together most of the anti-Indira elements. Whether this anti-Indira feeling can be translated into positive action remains to be seen. Some observers doubt the coalition can hold together long enough to successfully attack the pressing problems facing the Indian people. Perhaps democracy, as Prime Minister Morarji Desai boasts, has been restored. But the verdict has yet to be rendered as to how successfully the new coalition can govern. Inflation, unemployment, and strikes are again on the rise. The food coffers are full for the first time in a decade, but the old needs and problems remain. They must soon be addressed, for they grow more acute with each passing day.

The major problems of India today still center on food and population. India must curtail her birthrate or face starvation on a scale almost beyond human imagination. Births remain fairly constant at 39 per 1000, while the death rate has lowered over the years to 15 per 1,000. Thus every single year 24 per 1,000 (or 2.4%) are added to her millions, more than the entire population of Pennsylvania. Mrs. Gandhi had pushed family planning energetically. Everywhere posters attest to the desirability of the two-child family. Railway stations throughout the nation have set aside space for vasectomy clinics, and community action and development programs educate women about birth control. But the future of these programs under new leadership is in doubt. Increase in life expectancy and a lack of funds and medical personnel to staff family planning clinics have all but wiped out previous gains. Even the much-heralded "Green Revolution" brought about by the development of "miracle rice" and "miracle wheat" strains has not been able to feed India. India is still too dependent on the monsoon rains for survival, and in the last ten years they have been insufficient. There was widespread famine in 1966-1967 when these failed and again in 1976. India needs more than anything else a respite from the spiraling cycle of life which threatens her very being. Hopefully the new leadership can provide it.

Suggestions for Further Reading

Ahmad, Aziz, *Studies in Islamic Culture in the Indian Environment* (1964).

Basham, L.S., *The Wonder That Was India* (1963)

Bolitho, Hector, *Jinnah: Creator of Pakistan* (1964)

Bondurant, Joan, *Conquest of Violence: The Gandhian Philosophy of Conflict* (1961)

Brecher, Michael, *Nehru: A Political Biography* (1962)

Broomfield, J.H., *Elite Conflict in a Plural Society: Twentieth-Century Bengal* (1968)

Brown, W. Norman, *The United States and India, Pakistan, Bangladesh* (1972)

Chandra, Bipan, *The Rise and Growth of Economic Nationalism in India* (1966)

Collet, Sophia Dobson, *The Life and Letters of Raja Rammohun Roy* (1962)

Davies, C. Collin, *An Historical Atlas of the Indian Subcontinent* (1963)

de Bary, Wm. Theodore (ed.), *Sources of Indian Tradition* (1958)

Embree, Ainslie T., *Charles Grant and British Rule in India* (1962)

_____ , *India in 1857: Mutiny or War of Independence?* (1963)

_____ , *India's Search for National Identity* (1972)

Fischer, Louis, *The Essential Gandhi: His Life, Work, and Ideas* (1962)

Gandhi, Mohandas K., *An Autobiography: The Story of My Experiments With Truth* (1957)

Gordon, Leonard A., *Bengal: The Nationalist Movement: 1876-1940* (1974)

Greenberger, Allen J., *The British Image of India* (1969)

Harrison, Selig S., *India: The Most Dangerous Decades* (1960)

Heimsath, Charles H., *Indian Nationalism and Hindu Social Reform* (1964)

Irshick, Eugene F., *Politics and Social Conflict in South India* (1969)

Jones, Kenneth W., *Arya Dharm: Hindu Consciousness in 19th-Century Punjab* (1976)

Karve, D. D., (ed.), *The New Brahamans: Five Maharashtrian Families* (1963)

Kopf, David, *British Orientalism and the Bengal Renaissance: The Dynamics of Indian Modernization, 1773-1835* (1969)

Majumdar, R. D., *History of the Freedom Movement in India,* 3 vols. (1962-1963)

Menon, V. P., *Transfer of Power in India* (1957)

Metcalf, Thomas R., *The Aftermath of Revolt: India. 1857-1870* (1965)

Nehru, Jawaharlal, *The Discovery of India,* R. I. Crane (ed.) (1960)

───────── , *Toward Freedom* (1958)

Panikkar, K. M., *Asia and Western Dominance* (1959)

Philips, C. H. (ed.), *The Evolution of India and Pakistan, 1858-1947: Select Documents* (1962)

Rosselli, John, *Lord William Bentinck: Making of a Liberal Imperialist* (1974)

Rudolph, Lloyd I., and Rudolph, Suzanne H., *The Modernity of Tradition: Political Development in India* (1967)

Singh, Khushwant, *Train to Pakistan* (1956)

Smith, Donald E., *India as a Secular State* (1963)

Smith, Vincent A., *The Oxford History of India,* Percival Spear (ed.) (1967)

Srinivas, M. N., *Social Change in Modern India* (1967)

Stokes, Eric., *The English Utilitarians and India* (1959)

Wolpert, Stanley A., *Tilak and Gokhale: Revolution and Reform in the Making of Modern India* (1962)

───────── , *India* (1965)

Glossary

ahimsa — Ancient doctrine of not injuring living things.

Aryan — Ambiguous term for branch of Indo-European peoples who invaded India in 1700 B.C.

Battle of Plassey — In perspective, battle between Clive and Nawab of Bengal in 1757 which was won by the English and initiated the British conquest of India.

bazaar — Market place in Urdu language.

Bentinck Era — Period of 1828-35, when Anglicist socio-cultural policies prevailed.

Brahmo Samaj — An important movement within the modern Hindu world which pioneered a new and dynamic Hinduism.

Buddhism — Reformation ideology attributed to the Buddha (6th century B.C.) and aimed at ridding Aryan religion of its violent, orthodox, and unethical abuses.

Calcutta — Capital of British India from 1772-1911.

Communalist — Term used to designate one who seems interested solely in the welfare of his community, be it Hindu or Muslim.

Cornwallis, Lord Charles — Former British general in the American Revolution, who was Governor General of India, 1786-1793, and known for his westernized solutions to problems of Indian administration.

dasyu — Most likely, the Aryan term of disrepute for original Indian inhabitants.

Delhi — Capital of India (1206-1529). New Delhi, a 20th-century city built adjacent to the old, has been the capital for the past half century.

dharma — Core concept of classical Indian ethics based on duty to the occupational grouping to which one belongs. Later reinterpreted to mean religion.

Dravidian Languages — The indigenous languages of South India.

British East India Company — Controlled and ruled much of India from 1772-1857. Company originally chartered in England in 1600 by Queen Elizabeth I.

Harijans — Name Mohandas K. Gandhi liked to use for the untouchables or scheduled classes. Means the "Children of God." The term is today widely used in India.

hartal — Political technique popularized by Mohandas K. Gandhi which attempts to force suspension of all economic activity.

Hastings, Warren — First Company Governor General in 1772, who tried to establish order out of chaos by compelling company servants to study Indian languages and become responsive to the people whom they ruled.

Hindi — The modern tongue or language more directly related to ancient Sanskrit. Hindi is the mother-tongue of nearly one-third of the population.

Hindu Renaissance — Hindu response to intrusive impact of British colonialism and imperialism. A Hindu intellegentsia appears which seeks ways of reforming existing abuses in Hinduism and finding a new identity for a revitalized India in the modern world.

Islam — Religion of second largest community in India. Based on the scriptural source known as *Quran* and first articulated by the prophet Muhammad.

Jati System — Basic social unit among Hindus founded on specialized occupational activities and/or kinship groups.

jizya — Special tax on non-Muslim-governed country.

karma — Good and bad deeds which determine rebirth.

masjid — Mosque or place of worship for Muslims.

mandir — The Hindu temple or place of worship.

moksha — One of several Hindu concepts denoting the ultimate goal of salvation.

Mughal Dynasty — Rulers of India from early 16th century to the rise of the British raj in the late 18th century. Akbar is considered the eclectic architect of the empire, while Aurangzeb, who died in 1707, is looked upon as the bigoted emperor who hastened its decline.

Muslim — a believer in Islam.

nirvana — Buddhist equivalent of moksha.

Orientalist-Anglicist controversy — Conflict between values and attitudes by British officials in India on how best to improve Indian institutions, traditions, and beliefs. Orientalists favored policies which were based on Indian linguistic and cultural models, whereas Anglicists chose the westernized models.

Pali — The language of the Buddhists.

Parsi — Indian word for Persian. Minority community in India which professes Zoroastrianism, the pre-Islamic faith of Iran.

Rajputs – Feudal-like warrior dynasties of western India.

Sanskrit – Classical language of north India. Modern languages of north India are derived from Sanskrit as many modern European languages are derived from Latin.

Satyagraha – Name Mohandas K. Gandhi gave to his movement. Means literally the force of truth.

Sikhism – New religion based on fusion of components of Hinduism and Islam. Adherents located mostly in the Punjab.

Sultan – A Muslim (Moslem) title used by medieval conquerors and rulers whose headquarters were in or near Delhi.

Swaraj – What many Indian leaders, including Mohandas K. Gandhi, promised to followers. Can be and was variously interpreted to mean freedom, self-government, status within the empire.

Taj Mahal – Magnificent marble tomb built by Shah Jahan, a Mughal ruler, for his favorite wife, who died in childbirth.

Upanishads – One of the six classical schools of Indian philosophy which constituted a reaction against Brahmanical orthodoxy between 900-600 B.C.

Urdu – *Lingua franca* of Mughal India and official language of Pakistan.

Varna System – Fourfold stratification of Aryan society into warriors, priests, merchants, and cultivators.

Vedas – Earliest scriptural sources of the Aryans, later appropriated by the Hindus.

Zamindari System – The introduction into Bengal (1793) of the private property principle by which former tax collectors or zamindars became land owners.

Index